SERMONS FOR THE CHRISTIAN YEAR

Published @ 2017 Trieste Publishing Pty Ltd

ISBN 9780649701957

Sermons for the Christian Year by H. L. Goudge

Edited by Trieste Publishing Pty Ltd.
Cover @ 2017

www.triestepublishing.com

H. L. GOUDGE

SERMONS FOR THE CHRISTIAN YEAR

 Trieste

SERMONS FOR
THE CHRISTIAN YEAR

Sermons for
The Christian Year

By the
REV. H. L. GOUDGE, D.D.
Canon of Christ Church, Oxford
*Regius Professor of Divinity in
Oxford University*

SECOND IMPRESSION

London:
SKEFFINGTON & SON, LTD.
Paternoster House, St. Paul's, E.C.4

MADE AND PRINTED IN GREAT BRITAIN
AT GAINSBOROUGH PRESS, ST. ALBANS
BY FISHER, KNIGHT AND CO., LTD

PREFACE

THE sermons included in this volume have mostly been preached in Cathedral Churches. One is a University Sermon, but the rest have no academic character. I have tried first to select sermons which contain either thoughts, or ways of expressing thoughts, that may not be familiar ; and, secondly, to avoid subjects with which I have dealt in earlier books.

H. L. G.

CONTENTS

CONTENTS

SERMONS FOR
THE CHRISTIAN YEAR

THE KINGDOM, PRESENT AND FUTURE

The First Sunday in Advent

"The night is far spent, and the day is at hand : let us therefore cast off the works of darkness, and let us put on the armour of light."—Rom. xiii. 12.

It is a familiar situation which St. Paul here describes to us. The day has not yet dawned, for the sun rises late on these December mornings. But we must not wait for the light, as we do in summer. It is high time to cast off the coverings of the night, and to clothe ourselves for the work which the day will bring. And yet is this, spiritually interpreted, all that St. Paul means ? See how he continues. "Let us walk honestly, as in the day." No longer does he speak of the day as about to dawn : it has dawned already. Temperance, purity, humility, and love, of which he proceeds to speak, are not virtues which will soon be asked of us ; we must practise them now. So it is with his final demand of us, the putting on of the Lord Jesus Christ. We are not to wait for it till God's kingdom has come in its final glory, but to do it now. What, then, is St. Paul's real meaning ? Does the dawn of the kingdom of God lie altogether in the future, or is the darkness, as St. John expresses it, already "passing away," and "the true light" already shining ?

I

Now we have here an example of a difficulty which often meets us in the Bible. "The kingdom of God," that great blessing of which we read so often—what, are we to understand by it? Is it a blessing altogether of the future, and for which we must wait until the Lord's return, or is it a blessing which is ours already, and whose possession, more than aught else, should distinguish Christians from other men? Our Lord's own language is at first sight perplexing. As a rule, when He uses the phrase, He seems to be thinking of the future, "Not every one that saith unto me, Lord, Lord, shall enter into the kingdom of heaven; but he that doeth the will of my Father which is in heaven. Many will say to me in that, Lord, Lord, did we not prophesy by thy name, and by thy name cast out devils, and by thy name do many mighty works? And then will I profess unto them, I never knew you; depart from me, ye that work iniquity." And yet He also says, "If I by the Spirit of God cast out devils, then is the kingdom of God come upon you"; and again, "The kingdom of God cometh not with observation; neither shall they say, Lo, here! or There! for lo, the kingdom of God is in the midst of you." So it is also with the teaching of the Apostles. Always they are looking and longing for the Lord's return; and their converts are warned that, if they still practise heathen wickedness, they will not inherit the kingdom of God. Here, plainly, the kingdom lies in the future. And yet St. Paul can say that God has "delivered us out of the power of darkness, and translated us into the kingdom of the Son of his love"; and that "the kingdom of God is . . . righteousness, and peace, and joy in the Holy Ghost." Here, equally plainly, the kingdom of God already exists in the present. What is the solution of this difficulty?

The answer, I would suggest, lies here. The kingdom of God means the sovereignty, or rule, of God; and so there are different stages in its development. In a true sense, the kingdom came, when the Lord came. In Him, who always did the Father's will, the rule of God was already realized. Where He was, the kingdom was ; and to be attached to Him was to share in it and receive its blessings. But, when the Lord had died and been glorified, the kingdom of God came with new power in the coming of the Holy Ghost. The Holy Ghost is the earnest of our heavenly inheritance. Just in so far as His rule is accepted, the kingdom for us has come. But there is still much for which to look. As yet the true members of the kingdom are the few rather than the many. The world outside still lies in darkness ; even in the Church, neither corporately nor individually, are we yet fully obedient to the Spirit ; and even if we were, we should still find our bodies and our outward circumstances real hindrances to the life that we desire. Though the kingdom was at hand when the Baptist proclaimed it, and in a true sense in the Church has come, we are still in a true sense waiting and longing for it.

Thus there is no inconsistency in the language of the Lord and the Apostles. The Church is the twilight of the kingdom. It seems dark, if we contrast it with the brightness of the life one day to be ours ; and we say "The night is far spent and the day is at hand." But if we contrast it with the darkness of the world outside, it seems light ; and we say, "Let us walk honestly, as in the day." There, you see, are two points of view, each true and each valuable ; and, as St. Paul's words show, the practical call is the same in either case. Shall we think of them in turn this morning ? One has been most natural in some periods of the Church's life, and the other in others. One is most natural to the old, and the other to the young. Let us try to see the truth in both, and let the one supplement the other.

II

We begin then with St. Paul's first thought. It is dark yet, but the dawn is coming. This present life with its sin, its suffering, its sorrow, is not the life that God permanently intends for us. There is "an inheritance incorruptible, and undefiled, and that fadeth not away, a salvation ready to be revealed in the last time." That is specially the standpoint of St. Peter, the apostle of hope ; and it has been the prevailing standpoint in all ages of special suffering and strain. So it was in the age of the Apostles, when the old policy of Israel was going down in darkness and blood. So it was in St. Augustine's day, when the barbarians were over-running the Roman Empire, and the old civilization was perishing. So it was in the dark days of the 12th century.

"*Hora novissima, tempora persima sunt, vigilemus.*"

So it was sometimes with ourselves in the Great War.

Always there was joy in Christian hearts, the joy of the Holy Ghost ; but it arose chiefly out of faith in the great future prepared for us. "Rejoice in the Lord alway : again I will say Rejoice. The Lord is at hand." He is coming, and perhaps soon. That view is a right one, specially for the old, whose work will soon be over ; it rests upon the clear and reiterated teaching of the Lord Himself. Christians may often have been mistaken about the time of the final consummation ; it was not for the Apostles to know the times and seasons, which the Father had set within His own authority ; and, if not for them, also not for us. But, though Christians have often been mistaken about the time, they have not been mistaken about the fact. Do we not need to-day to renew our faith in the Lord's promise ? It is said that the old Advent hymns are no longer sung, and that many miss them. But why should we cease to sing them ? They are written, no doubt, in the bold symbolic language of Hebrew prophecy ; and the language of symbol is not the language of exact knowledge. It is the way, and perhaps the only way, in which truths can be expressed which are too far beyond us to be apprehended as they are. But symbols are given us to express truth, not falsehood. Which will at last find himself the more mistaken, the simple Christian who believes that Christ will come riding upon visible clouds, and sit upon a visible throne of judgment, or the Christian who, because he cannot literally understand such words as these, has ceased to believe that the Lord will return at all ? An ever-changing world that had no end would have no meaning, since it is only when the end is reached that we see the meaning of all that has led to it. To think of this life as all is to misunderstand our Father's love ; the true life lies beyond.

What then are we to say of this present world ? From this point of view it is a "vale of soul-making" ; our life here is a life of discipline, of training, of probation for another life hereafter to be revealed. That is why it is high time to awake out of sleep ; to cast off the works of darkness, and put on the armour of light. That we should eat and drink and make the most of all bodily pleasures is natural if "to-morrow we die" ; but not natural if to-morrow we begin truly to live.

But though that is St. Paul's first, it is not, as we have seen, his only thought. For, though there is a great future, there is a great present also. The Kingdom of God has come with power already in the coming of the Holy Spirit ; and all life must be consecrated and made lovely by His presence. That is the point of view of happy days when the Church has peace : "and, walking in the fear of the Lord, and the comfort of the Holy Ghost, is multiplied." It is, and ought to be, dominant with the young. We should not think of our life here only as preparation and probation for another beyond. If it is guided and blessed by the Spirit of God, it has a present value and beauty of its own. "Whatsoever things are true, whatsoever things are just, whatsoever things are pure, whatsoever things are of good report ; if there be any virtue, and if there be any praise," we are to take account of them all, and "adorn the doctrine of God our Saviour in all things." The world is not only a vale of soul-making, but a vale of service. The Church is God's missionary to the world ; and her mission must be proved, as was the mission of the Lord Himself, by the promised blessings of the

B

kingdom she proclaims being already brought near in her
life and activity. "Art thou he that should come, or do
we look for another?" It is the facts which must answer.
"The blind receive their sight, and the lame walk, the lepers
are cleansed, and the deaf hear, the dead are raised up, and
the poor have the gospel preached to them." From this
point of view also, how moving is St. Paul's call! "Revel-
ling and drunkenness, chambering and wantonness"—
these things are so evil, not only because those who live
in them will not inherit God's kingdom in the future, but
because they forfeit God's kingdom here and now, and the
joy which it brings. "Strife and envying" are so evil
not only because they will shut us out from God's future
kingdom of love, but because a Church divided against
itself cannot manifest the present rule of God, and disgusts
the world rather than attracts it. Once more, we are to put
on the Lord Jesus Christ, not only because it is His character
alone that will fit us for the future kingdom, but because it
is the only character for us here and now, and we can never
do His will without it.

III

My brothers, there are these two points of view; which
shall be our own? God helping us, we will accept both. So
the hearts of the fathers will be turned to the children, and
the hearts of the children to the fathers; and old and young
will put on Christ together. The old will say, "My working
days are over now; I was young once, but now am old,
though one day the Lord will make me young again. I
watch and wait for His coming. I do not understand all
that the young are saying and doing; what is Toc H?
And who is Mr. Buchman? Sometimes the young seem to
me to be forgetting the Gospel, to think that they can build
God's kingdom for themselves, and out of people who
have not learned to love Him. But I daresay there is
more in what they say and do than I can understand."

And the young will say, "My working days are now.
I must work the works of Him who sends me while it is

day ; the night cometh when no man can work. I do not trouble much about the Lord's Second Advent ; I want to make something of His First. My father thinks about the many mansions : I think about the many slums. If we preach the Gospel to those that live in them, they "hearken not for anguish of spirit and for cruel bondage." But I daresay that there is more in the Second Advent than I can understand. Perhaps I may grow tired of trying to build the kingdom here, unless I remember that there is more beyond it."

"On the earth the broken arcs ; in the heaven a perfect round."

And both will say, though perhaps for different reasons, that now it is high time to awake out of sleep ; and pray for a closer union with the living Christ.

> "O quickly come, great King of all ;
>   Reign all around us, and within ;
> Let sin no more our souls enthrall,
>   Let pain and sorrow die with sin ;
> O quickly come : for Thou alone
> Can'st make Thy scattered people one."

SERMON II

THE JUDGMENTS OF GOD

THE SECOND SUNDAY IN ADVENT

"Upon the earth distress of nations, with perplexity ;
the sea and the waves roaring ; men's hearts failing them
for fear, and for looking after those things which are
coming on the earth ; for the powers of heaven shall be
shaken. And then shall they see the Son of man coming
in a cloud, with power and great glory. And when these
things begin to come to pass, then look up, and lift up
your heads ; for your redemption draweth nigh."—
LUKE xxi. 25-28.

STRANGE words these, to come from the lips of the Lord !
"Where," we say, "is His pity ? Where is His compassion
for the sufferings of men ?" It is a terrible picture which
the Lord here draws. The great deep of human society
is broken up ; the powers which control it seem tottering
to their fall. "Upon the earth" there is "distress of nations
with perplexity." "Men's hearts" are "failing them for
fear, and for looking after those things which are coming
on the earth." And yet what says our Lord ? "When
these things begin to come to pass, then look up, and lift
up your heads ; for your redemption draweth nigh." It
is summer that is coming in. "Behold the fig-tree, and
all the trees ; when they now shoot forth, ye see and know
of your own selves that summer is now nigh at hand."
The anguish of the world is the travail-pang that ushers in
the new life. The Church is to look to the end, and lift up
her head, when she sees it approaching.

I

I would speak to you this morning of that "distress of
nations with perplexity," of which our minds are full at
this present time. Now as ever, when men's hearts are

failing them for fear, the Church is to look up, and lift up her head. And why so? Because the Church can look beyond the distress. "In quietness and confidence" is her strength. Christian hope is a sure and certain hope. It is the sure confidence that God will do what God has promised. But hope as St. Paul reminds us in this day's Epistle, requires patience and comfort of the Scriptures, if she is to live. "Whatsoever things were written aforetime, were written for our learning; that we through patience and comfort of the Scriptures might have hope." Shall we look then to-day at some part of this comfort of the Scriptures, that hope may grow strong, even in face of present facts?

Our Lord, no doubt, in the chapter from which these words are taken, is speaking primarily of the approaching doom of Jerusalem, and of the way in which His Apostles are to regard it. But His words nevertheless have far more than a historical interest; they have an interest for every generation, and for every human soul. Our Lord here speaks as the greatest of the prophets; and, like the prophets of the Old Testament and St. John, the prophet of the New Testament, in interpreting the history of His time, He shows us how to interpret that of our own. The prophets ever deal with the real world; the misery and confusion, the war, famine, and pestilence, of which they speak, are the misery and confusion, the war, famine, and pestilence, of which our papers inform us. What they show is us the sources from which these things spring, the principles of the divine government which they exemplify, the purposes which they serve, and the end to which they are tending. So really is this the case with St. John, that men have often sought to interpret his Apocalypse as an inspired prediction of the whole course of history from his time until the end of the world. And, although this view of the book is clearly erroneous, it has this large measure of truth in it. Just because it is ever the same God who rules human history, and just because the principles by which He rules it are ever the same, history is ever repeating itself. What St. John says of the events of his own time applies to the events of many other times. Thus there is a sense in which it is true to say that the Great War is in the Revelation of St. John, and that the Russian Revolution is there, and that the present financial problems of the world are there. It is not that there are texts in that book which refer to these things, and to nothing else ; it is simply that these things are admirable illustrations of the universal principles of God's government. We can understand them by the words of our Lord and of the prophets, as we can understand them in no other way. What we need to do is not to turn our eyes away from the real world to some unreal "religious" world of our own, but to bring the divine light to bear upon the real world, that in that light we may understand it. Then its events, instead of perplexing our faith, will strengthen it ; instead of overwhelming us, they will lift us up.

II

What then do our Lord and the prophets see as they look out into the world ! First, they see the great world-kingdoms, the great world-empires. Secondly, they see the Church of God, sometimes comparatively faithful to Him, sometimes appallingly unfaithful. Thirdly, when the Church is thus appallingly unfaithful, they see—amid the world-empires, amid the visible Church, but distinguished from both—a "little flock," the true servants of God. These are the visible actors in the world's drama, and it is with their mutual relations that our Lord and the prophets deal. In our Lord's prophecy, from which to-day's Gospel is taken, the three appear quite clearly. Here the world-empire is the world-empire of Rome, whose armies our Lord sees hovering upon the horizon ; the apostate Church is the Jewish people ; and the little flock is that of our Lord's personal followers. In the Revelation of St. John the same three actors reappear. First, there is the world-empire of Rome, the wild beast "having ten

horns and seven heads, and on his horns ten crowns, and
upon his head names of blasphemy." It is the Rome which
has beheaded St. Paul and crucified St. Peter, which has
covered Christians with pitch and burned them in her
gardens, and whose Emperors claim divine honours from
all their subjects. Secondly, there is apostate Jerusalem,
"Babylon the Great," the harlot-city, which rests not upon
God, but upon the "scarlet-coloured beast" of Rome.*
Terrible in its truth was this description. The rulers of
the nation had declared that they had no king but Cæsar ;
they had given up their king to the Cross, because they
feared that, if they let Him alone, the Romans would come
and take away their place and nation. Thirdly, over
against these, and persecuted by both, there is "the bride,
the Lamb's wife," the little band of those who "follow the
Lamb whithersoever he goeth." These were the actors in
St. John's day, and the actors are still essentially the same.
First, there are the great world-kingdoms—Russia, Germany, France, England, and the rest. Secondly, there is
the visible Church, sometimes faithful, sometimes unfaithful. Thirdly, there is the little band of those who live by
the Church's true principles, and follow the Lamb whithersoever he goes. But have we enumerated all the actors ?
No, we have omitted the chief. The chief is God, no
impartial spectator of the world's drama, but the chief
actor in it—God, who sits above the water-floods, judging
all, dealing with all in perfect justice and love, and patiently
working for that divine kingdom, which the world is at
last to see. How then does God judge the world ? Not
how will He one day judge it, but how does He judge it
even now ? According as each other actor answers to His
purposes, forwards his kingdom or forwards it not. The
kingdoms of the world and the Church of Christ have not
the same task ; each has its own. God judges them by
their performances of it.

---

*Note.—In the original form of the prophecy Babylon seems to
have stood for apostate Jerusalem, though, as we read the Apocalypse to-day, it probably stands for Rome.

What then is the task of the kingdoms of the world ?
A high and noble one—the maintenance of natural justice.
It is not the work of the kingdoms of the world to forward
God's kingdom directly—that is the task of the Church.
It is their work to forward it indirectly by maintaining
natural justice against the evil-doers within their borders,
and the foreign aggressors without, and so by securing that
fair field within which the Church may work.   That surely
is the teaching of St. Paul and of St. Peter. "There is no
power but of God ; and the powers that be are ordained of
God. . . .   Rulers are not a terror to the good work, but to
the evil."   The civil magistrate is the "minister of God"
to us for good. . . .   "He beareth not the sword in vain :
for he is a minister of God, an avenger for wrath to him
that doeth evil."   That is the task of the kingdoms of the
world, and, as far as I see, they have no other.   Do not let
us be misled by that beautiful phrase "a Christian country."
There are no Christian countries—would that there were !
The New Testament seems to teach us that there never
will be.   The kingdoms of the world become the kingdoms
of the Lord and of His Christ, when the Lord returns and
not before.   There are countries with more, or with fewer,
Christian inhabitants than others, but that is all.   The
establishment of the Church does not alter the fact.   The
corporate action of a nation can never be fully Christian,
because that action can never, if it is to be effective, go far
beyond the average opinion of its citizens.   What is
asked of the kingdoms of the world is that they should
maintain those principles of natural justice, which all men
are able to understand ; and God judges them according as
they do, or do not, carry out this duty.   Why then, to
take but one example, should we wonder at the Russian
revolution ?   I know that Russia claimed to be a Christian
country, and possessed an established Church.   But God
judges by practice, not by profession, and it requires more
than an established Church to blind His eyes.   The
government of Russia maintained justice neither within
its own borders, nor beyond them. Its rulers were frequently

a terror to the good work, not only to the evil. Its foreign policy was a policy of lying and injustice. Thus, from God's point of view, it bore the sword in vain, and He swept it away. Would you know the method ? We may read it in the history of the last fifteen years, or we may read it in the Revelation of St. John. Both say the same thing. "And I saw when the Lamb opened one of the seven seals, and I heard one of the four living creatures saying as with a voice of thunder, Come. And I saw, and behold, a white horse, and he that sat thereon had a bow ; and there was given unto him a crown : and he came forth conquering and to conquer. And when he opened the second seal, I heard the second living creature saying, Come. And another horse came forth, a red horse : and to him that sat thereon it was given to take peace from the earth, and that they should slay one another : and there was given unto him a great sword. And when he opened the third seal, I heard the third living creature saying, Come. And I saw, and behold, a black horse : and he that sat thereon had a balance in his hand. And I heard as it were a voice in the midst of the four living creatures saying, a measure of wheat for a denarius and three measures of barley for a denarius. . . . And when he opened the fourth seal, I heard the voice of the fourth living creature saying, Come. And I saw, and behold, a pale horse : and he that sat upon him, his name was Death ; and Hades followed with him." The programme was strictly followed. First, the white horse of foreign war. Next, the red horse of civil strife. Next, the black horse of famine. Last, the pale horse of death. Pray we indeed for Russia ; her people have suffered terribly, and the end is not yet. But do not let us ascribe her fall to any but the right causes or fail to take warning ourselves.

We pass to the second actor in the world's drama—the visible Church of Christ. What is her task—the task of the whole Church, and of every part of it ? It is to forward the kingdom of God directly. It is to represent in the world Jesus Christ in His prophetic, His priestly, and His regal work. The Church is to be the inspired prophet to call men to repentance and faith, to reveal to them God and their own destiny. She is to be the priest of the world, to intercede for it, and unite it to God. She is to be the viceroy of Jesus Christ, to discipline men's lives according to His law. And she is to be all this by bold witness and patient suffering, following the Lamb whithersoever He goes. Never may she accept the world's standards; never may she work by the world's methods. The civil governor "bears not the sword in vain"—he is to use it. The place of the Church's sword is in its sheath. "Put up thy sword into the sheath." "All they that take the sword shall perish by the sword." Thus the Church must rest upon God alone. Perfectly friendly she should be to the nations of the world, as they do their work, and helpful to them by every means within her power. Where no principle forbids, she should "give to him that asketh her;" from the nation that "would borrow of" her, she should "turn not away." If the nation would "take away" her "coat," it can have her "cloke also." If it compels her to "go with it a mile," she should "go with it twain." But all this, saving her principles. Never may she rest upon a kingdom of the world; never may she merge herself in it. The kingdoms of the world are never likely to accept the Church's ideals; if she merges herself in them, she loses her hold upon those ideals herself. But how easily we forget all this, clergy and laity alike! How easily we allow the voice of the Church to become a feeble echo of the voice of the nation or of the voice of the civil government! How lightly we barter our real influence for position and popularity, for what we suppose to be the opportunity of influence! So we become, not the city of God, but Babylon, resting, as in St. John's vision, not on God, but on a kingdom of the world, and doomed to perish by it, or to perish with it. Would you see the portrait of a national church of this kind? You will find it in the Revelation of St. John. He has depicted the Roman

Empire, and he goes on to depict the national religion of Rome. And what a picture it is ! It is the picture of a second wild beast only too like the first. "Horns" it has "like unto a lamb," for it is a religious power ; but it speaks, and its voice is a dragon's voice. "He exerciseth all the authority of the first beast in his sight. And he maketh the earth and them that dwell therein to worship the first beast." That is the picture of the apostate Church of all ages ; it is nothing if not patriotic. It is "the false prophet," glorifying the earthly power on which it rests, saying, "Who is like unto the beast ? and who is able to war with him ?" And, if we would know why the national Church of Russia, in the crisis of the nation's fate, seemed to be so powerless for good, and why those who hated and destroyed the Russian government also still hate and desire to destroy the Russian Church, we may find the answer in the way in which that Church had identified itself with the Russian government, had glorified it, and made men worship it, instead of calling it to repentance. As St. John tells us, "the beast and the false prophet" always go together to the abyss.

But where in all this is the hope of which our Lord speaks ? It lies where it ever lies, in the faithful "remnant," and in what God will certainly make of it. It is ever there, that faithful remnant, even in the worst times —"all the knees, which have not bowed unto Baal, and every mouth which hath not kissed him." It is there, and it will live and prosper. "Fear not, little flock ; for it is your Father's good pleasure to give you the kingdom." It is His good pleasure ; the kingdom will be given ; and the judgments on the world forward it. There are words which I omitted, as I read to you the description of God's judgments. "The oil and the wine hurt thou not." Oil and wine are the symbols of the blessings of the people of God. "Thou hast anointed my head with oil ; my cup runneth over." The blessings of the people of God are ever perfectly safe ; and, whether on earth or in Paradise, they themselves are safe to enjoy them. Meanwhile, in

patience and comfort of the Scriptures they must have
hope ; their day will come. "They shall hunger no more,
neither thirst any more ; neither shall the sun strike upon
them, nor any heat ; for the Lamb which is in the midst
of the throne shall be their shepherd, and shall guide them
unto fountains of waters of life : and God shall wipe away
every tear from their eyes."

III

My brothers, need I draw the lesson ?   You can draw it
for yourselves.   Russia yesterday, Germany to-day, England perhaps to-morrow. "Wheresoever the carcase is,
there will the vultures be gathered together." Wheresoever there is a rotting society, wheresoever there is cruelty
and avarice and injustice, there, sooner or later, and
probably very soon, the judgments of God will be seen in
the world, "that the inhabitants of the world may learn
righteousness." We do not wish it otherwise. We say
with St. John, "Even so, Amen." "Great and marvellous
are Thy works, O Lord God, the Almighty ; righteous and
true are Thy ways, Thou King of the Ages." Do you think
that society in England, apart from the character of our
people, is more stable than in other countries ? It is far
less stable. In a country like France, where the land is in
the hands of the people, society is stable, though govern-
ments may not be so : the great body of the people have
something to lose. But the vast majority of our own
people live from hand to mouth, and have next to nothing
to lose. In France, as in Russia, there is a large army,
with the habit of obedience. In England there is not.
English society rests upon moral principles, upon the sense
of a common interest and a common life, upon the traditional kindness of the rich to the poor, upon the greater
kindness and forbearance of the poor to the rich. Character
is our all ; where are we, if we allow it to decay ? And
character can only be maintained by effort, and that
Christian effort. It is idle to address our exhortations to

the nation as a whole. It is the Church, which must be active, clergy and laity alike, in that fair field which the nation gives her. "When the best men cease trying," it has been well said, "the world sinks back like lead." Let us pray for our nation, for the country where we dwell. "In its peace shall" we "have peace." Let us pray for our government, that it may do justice within and beyond our borders, for that is what God asks of it. But do not let us expect too much of our country or of our government. If character is to be maintained, it is we Christians who must maintain it. We must hold up the Christian, and not merely the national ideal ; we must live by it, and be ready to suffer for it. As this Advent the words of Isaiah and of the Revelation of St. John are read to us, let us listen to the message they convey. "Heaven and earth" may "pass away," but the Lord's word will "not pass away."

THE THREE JUDGMENTS

The Third Sunday in Advent

"Let a man so account of us, as of Ministers of Christ and stewards of the mysteries of God. Here, moreover, it is required in stewards that a man be found faithful. But with me it is a very small thing that I should be judged of you, or of man's judgment : yea, I judge not mine own self. For I know nothing against myself ; yet am I hereby justified : but He that judgeth me is the Lord."—I Cor. iv. 1-4.

WHAT a grand simplicity it would give to our lives, if only we could remember this ! Servants and stewards—yes ! that is what we are, clergy and laity alike. Our ministry and service may not all be of the same character ; the gifts and powers of which we are stewards vary greatly ; we are to be "good stewards", as St. Peter says, "of the manifold grace of God." But servants and stewards we all alike are, with the servant's responsibility and no more. What is required of us is that we should be found faithful—not brilliant, not even outwardly successful, but just faithful. Then our Master's care is sure from beginning to end of our service, and sure too His praise at the end.

But it is not to the first words of the text that I would chiefly direct your thoughts to-day. It is rather to those later words, in which St. Paul speaks of the various judgments to which we are exposed, and teaches us their comparative importance, and the attention we should give to each of them. We all are judged, clergy and laity alike, and we all judge other people. Indeed, I think we should be surprised, if we examined the matter, to find how much of our thoughts, and perhaps of our words, is occupied by judgments passed upon other people. We may judge

harshly, or we may judge generously, but at least we judge.
Moreover, the fact that this is so is a fact ever present to
our minds. We may say that we do not care what others
think of us, but the fact is otherwise. We care a great
deal, and cannot help caring. It is the appreciation and
respect of others which make a great part of our happiness,
and their neglect or contempt a great part of our pain.
Thus it is surely well that we should consider these profound
words of St. Paul. There are, as he says, three judgments
which we have all to face. There is the judgment of
others, and that is a very small thing ; there is our own
judgment upon ourselves, and that, if we are honest, is a
much greater thing ; and then beyond both there will be
the judgment of our Lord Himself, and that is far the
greatest. Shall we think then of these three judgments
to-day ? Each has its value ; each needs to be continually
remembered ; but we need to put them in the right order,
and assign to each its right measure of importance.

I

We begin then with the judgment which is the least
important, and that is the judgment which others form
about us. St. Paul says that that is a very little thing.
"With me it is a very small thing that I should be judged
of you, or of man's judgment." Now observe that, though
St. Paul says that it is a very small thing, he does not say
that it is valueless. On the contrary, it has a place of its
own, and we are right to think about it. I have heard of
a castle which had these words carved over its entrance-
gate, "They say. What do they say ? Let them say."
But be sure that these words are no Christian words. God
has made us to be dependent one upon another. He has
made us to find our happiness one in another. The man
who claims to stand alone, to be independent of the judgment and goodwill of those among whom he lives, is a man
who claims to be what he never can be, and what God
never intended him to be. Never despise the good opinion

of anybody ; never lose it by your own fault. St. Paul
warns Timothy that the Christian presbyter must have
"good testimony from them that are without."   If he have
it not, he may "fall into reproach and the snare of the
devil."   You see how the Apostle values even heathen
opinion.   And if that be so, how much more ought we to
care for the opinion of our fellow-Christians whose consciences are enlightened by the Spirit of God ! How much
St. Paul cared for it for his work's sake, and for his own
loving heart's sake too ! He would not please men rather
than God, but he would ever please men rather than himself. He became all things to all men, that he might by
all means save some ; he commended himself to every man's
conscience in the sight of God. People say "never explain."
Infamous maxim of the world ! How in this world of
misunderstandings are we ever to maintain good will, if
we never explain ? St. Paul was never too proud to
explain, and to put himself right with those who had mis-
understood him. Never explain if your conduct will not
bear a truthful explanation ; always explain, if it will.
Listen always to the criticism of others. We can always
learn by it even though we may have to set it aside. The
judgment of others is of real importance. Only remember
at the same time that, important as it is, it is nevertheless
—comparatively—a very small thing, just because it can
never be entirely true. As St. Paul says, there are so
many hidden things of darkness, so many things about us
which others do not know, and cannot know, and which
yet would alter their judgment, if they did know them ;
the counsels of the hearts, the hidden motives from which
we act, are so very hidden, that it does not follow, because
the best people blame that God blames, or that because
the best people praise that God praises. Give the judgment
of others its due. After all—comparatively—it is a very
small thing.

We pass to the second type of judgment, and that is the
judgment which by the action of our consciences we
continually pass upon ourselves. That is a judgment far

more important than the judgment of others, both because
it comes so closely home to us, and because, if we are
honest, it is likely to be so much nearer to the truth.   The
American statesman, James Garfield, said that, let other
people think what they would of him, there was one man
whose good opinion he must have, for he had to eat with
him, walk with him, work with him, sleep with him, and
never be quit of him night or day, and that was James
Garfield himself.   It is so, is it not ?   We can do without
the approval of others, though it is difficult to do without
it, but we cannot do without our own.   Not only so, but, as
I said just now, the judgment which is passed upon ourselves is, if we are honest, likely to be for the most part a
true judgment, the nearest which in this world we shall
get to the judgment of God.   Of course the judgment of our
conscience is not the same as God's, and St. Paul says so.
He judges not his own self with any final and certain
judgment; and, even though he knows nothing against
himself, he is not for that reason certain of the approval
of God.   There are consciences—perhaps our own are
among them—which are very dull and unenlightened,
consciences which do not condemn though they ought to
condemn.   There are consciences again which are morbid
and diseased, consciences which condemn, though there is
no sound reason for condemning.   We have always to
remember with St. John that God is greater than our hearts,
and knows all things.   But nevertheless, though our consciences do not enable us to foresee God's judgment in its
entirety, they do enable us to foresee very much of it ;
and therefore we should never be satisfied while they are
not at rest.   St. Paul once said that he exercised himself
to have a conscience void of offence toward God and men
alway ;   and there is no form of exercise that is so necessary
to perfect health.   A burdened conscience is far too heavy
a handicap in the race of life for anyone to carry it without
the certainty of failure.   If your conscience is burdened,
see that by repentance and confession you lay that burden
down.   If your conscience is uneasy, if there are things

C

in your life whose lawfulness you doubt, seek advice about them. Pray God, either directly or by the ministry of others, to make His will clear, and to grant you courage and self-sacrifice to do it, whatever it may prove to be. If fuller light comes, do not reject it, or shut your eyes to it. You must know nothing against yourselves, if you are to be either happy or useful in your life here.

And now we pass to that final and mysterious judgment which our Lord will pass, when He judges us all: That, of course, is immeasurably the greatest and immeasurably the truest. "Judge nothing before the time, until the Lord come, who will both bring to light the hidden things of darkness, and make manifest the counsels of the hearts ; and then shall each man have his praise from God." My brothers, do you think that the thought of the last judgment means to us all that it meant to those who have gone before us in the faith ? I do not think that it does. Our "Lord delayeth His coming" ; and the picture language in which we speak of it is only picture language, as we know full well. But do we remember that though they are but pictures, they are pictures of a great reality, and that one day to each of us the judgment which our Lord will pass upon our lives, will be the greatest reality in the world ? Our Lord will not judge us harshly or unjustly. If others have done so here, we shall have justice from Him. But though He will never judge harshly, He will judge truly ; and we must so live now, that we can bear the truth which will come out then. The hidden things of darkness —the things that others knew not and could not know, the things which we ourselves once knew but have forgotten, the things about ourselves which in our carelessness we never noticed, and so never knew—they all will come out then. The counsels of our hearts, the hidden and complex motives from which we acted, there will be no hiding them then, or ourselves either. That is where, I think, a great hymn sometimes misleads us. Most true it is that we may hide ourselves now in the Rock of Ages who was cleft for us, that we may take refuge from our

sin in Him who can change us from what we are to what
He Himself would have us be. But most false it is, that,
when we see our Lord upon His judgment throne, we may
hide ourselves in the Rock of Ages.   Then we shall be seen
as we are, and judged as we are ; and, if the grace of our
Lord has not by then transformed us, He will not hide us
from Himself or from His Father either.   Very little it will
matter to us then what others have thought of us, or what
we may have thought of ourselves.   What will matter to us
then will be the judgment of our Lord, and whether we
have so lived as to be able to bear it.

II

So then, you see, there are these three judgments'
There is the judgment of others, and that is a very little
thing.   There is the judgment of our own consciences, and
that is a greater thing, because if we are honest, it is so
much truer.   But beyond them both there lies the judgment of our Lord, and that will be the truest and the
greatest of them all.   And what does it suggest to us that
St. Paul ends with the words, "Then shall every man have
praise of God."   Does it not suggest the beautiful thought
that He, before whom we shall stand, is One who would
far rather praise than blame, far rather say "Well done"
than say "Depart from Me "?   Who that has studied His
earthly life could ever doubt it ?   He tells us indeed that,
when we have done all, we are to say that we are unprofit-
able servants, and have but done that which it was our
duty to do.   Yes ! that is what we are to say, and who that
knows what the Lord has done for him could say anything
else ?   But is that what He Himself will say ?   Is He the
kind of Master who may indeed be just satisfied, but can
never be more, though we do for Him what we will. Listen
to the judgment from the Master's side, "Blessed are those
servants, whom the Lord when he cometh shall find
watching : verily I say unto you, that he shall gird himself, and make them to sit down to meat, and shall come

and serve them. Who then is the faithful and wise steward whom his Lord shall set over his household to give them their portion of food in due season ? Blessed is that servant whom his lord, when he cometh, shall find so doing. Of a truth I say unto you, that he will set him over all that he hath." Do you not think that, when St. Paul wrote, "Then shall every man have praise of God," these words of the Lord may have been in his mind ? Ministers and stewards, servants and stewards—he uses the same words which the Lord used. And if that be so, then he reminds us, as we go to our work, that we go out to serve the most generous and appreciative of masters, a Master who loves to praise us, and looks forward to praising us, and whose heart will be grieved if He must do anything else. He asks not of us the outward success that meets the eye—little enough in His earthly life He had of it Himself. What He asks of us, as St. Paul says, is faithfulness only—it is required in stewards that a man be found faithful—and who is there among us who cannot give Him that ?

AN ORDINATION SERMON

The Fourth Sunday in Advent

"Behold, I send unto you prophets, and wise men, and scribes ; some of them shall ye kill and crucify ; and some of them shall ye scourge in your synagogues and persecute from city to city. . . . O Jerusalem, Jerusalem, which killeth the prophets, and stoneth them that are sent unto her ! How often would I have gathered thy children together, even as a hen gathereth her chickens under her wings, and ye would not ! Behold, your house is left unto you desolate. For I say unto you, ye shall not see Me henceforth, till ye shall say, Blessed is he that cometh in the name of the Lord."—Matt. xxiii. 34, 37-39.

THERE are, brethren, in these words at once a profound sadness and an unfaltering determination. For Jerusalem thus far the love of God had been in vain. Ever that apostate city had killed her prophets, and stoned them that were sent unto her ; she would do it till the hour of her doom. But if Jerusalem can persist, God can persist also. "Prophets, and wise men, and scribes" He had sent in the past, and He would send them still. Through all man's obstinacy and violence His purpose holds. If the new messengers are rejected, judgment will fall ; the national life will pass away. But even so there is hope beyond. The Christ of God will even yet be accepted ; the time will come for the welcome, "Blessed is he that cometh in the Name of the Lord."

I

It may seem that I have chosen a strange and depressing text for an Ordination sermon. But it is only depressing if we mean to be unfaithful ; in itself it is full of hope and encouragement. It speaks to us of that unfailing purpose of God which no wilfulness can blunt, and no rejection tire out. It speaks of the ministry as the instrument of that purpose, and of the great issues for every nation and every man which hang upon the way in which the Word of God is received. And what is the purpose of God ? It is a purpose of gathering—a twofold gathering of men to God, and of men one to another.

"O Jerusalem, Jerusalem, how often would I have gathered thy children together, even as a hen gathereth her chickens under her wings, and ye would not !" Are we to take these last words, as some would have us take them, as referring to those hurried visits of our Lord to Jerusalem, of which we read in St. John's Gospel ? Surely not. Surely our Lord here speaks as the Eternal "Wisdom". That beautiful simile which He employs is an Old Testament simile for the sheltering care of God. "The Lord, the God of Israel, under whose wings thou art come to take refuge." "Keep me as the apple of the eye ; hide me under the shadow of thy wings."' It was He, our Lord, the Eternal Wisdom, who had sent the prophets, wise men, and scribes in the past—the prophets of the Old Testament dispensation, the wise men to whom we owe the Wisdom Literature, the scribes to whom, since they sat in Moses's seat, He had but just bidden the people to hearken—it was He who would send them still. Jesus is the gatherer. He came "to gather together into one the children of God that are scattered abroad," and, if we gather not with Him, we scatter.

Do not separate the two fellowships—fellowship with God and fellowship one with another. We are only truly gathered under the wings of God ; and, though the wings of God are wide wings, they will shelter no one who will not be a brother to his fellow men. The centre of human fellowship is God revealed in Christ, and the place of human fellowship is the Church. Outside the Church men scatter as fast as we gather them. "That which we have seen and heard," says St. John, "declare we unto you." And why ?

"That ye also may have fellowship with us." Boldly he says it. The purpose of Christian preaching is to gather men to the Church. Only, of course, he goes on, "Yea, and our fellowship is with the Father and with his Son, Jesus Christ." The Church gathers men to God by gathering them to herself, and she gathers men to herself by gathering them to God. There may be fellowships beyond founded upon common interests or common antipathies, the fellowship of one nation to fight another nation, or of one class to fight another class. But outside the Church there can be no universal fellowship. It is only under the wings of God that the rich and the poor meet together ; only there that there is neither Greek nor Jew, barbarian, Scythian, bondman, freeman : but Christ is all, and in all.

II

Thus far for the purpose ; now for the instruments. What a variety of instruments our Lord employs ! "Behold ! I send unto you prophets and wise men and scribes." So it was under the old dispensation, and so it is still. The minister of Christ must be all three in some measure, but in his teaching office he is generally, I think, predominantly one. Let us look in order at these three classes—we of the clergy to learn from the Lord what we are to be, you of the laity to learn from the Lord what you are to expect, all of us alike that we may learn something of the manifold wisdom of God, as He deals with us in view of the variety of our gifts and the variety of our circumstances.

There is first the prophet. "Behold ! I send unto you prophets." What is prophecy, and who is the prophet ? The prophet is the messenger ; he is the man who speaks for God a special message with which God has charged him at the time. It may be for a nation ; it may be for a Church ; it may be for a congregation ; it may even be for one special individual ; but ever it is a message with a special character of its own, a message to be spoken at the time and to the people for which it is intended. Thus the

prophet will seldom know his message much in advance ;
often he will have to wait for it ; sometimes it will be as
new to him as to those to whom he speaks it. Never can
he invent his message, or deliver an old message, unless
he is filled with it again. But it is given, and he waits no
longer. He is "stung with the splendour of a sudden
thought ;" and then thought follows thought, too fast
sometimes for tongue or pen to keep pace with them ; for
the time, like Saul among the prophets, he is changed into
another man. My brothers to be ordained to-day, God
may mean some of you to share in the gift of prophecy.
Again and again God may have special messages to deliver
through your lips to the people to whom He sends you.
Do not miss your calling, do not deprive your people of
what God would give, from refusal to live near to God
and to listen to His voice. "I will hear what God the Lord
will speak." That is the true prophetic attitude ; see that
you take it. It is the prophet who brings God nearest
to us. It is hard for the Church to live without prophecy ;
there is no famine so deadly as a "famine of hearing the
words of the Lord." And do you, my brothers of the
laity, listen to the word that God sends to you ; if you
reject it, you may never hear it again. But if you accept
it, if you receive a prophet in the name of a prophet, you
will receive a prophet's reward.

But the prophet is only one of the gifts of our Lord.
Behold, He sends unto us wise men also. Who then is the
wise man, and what is his wisdom ? The wise man is the
Christian scholar and thinker, the watchman on his tower
who surveys the field of truth. He is the man who brings
to us, not the special message for the special circumstances,
but the broad and general message of the whole Christian
faith. He is the man who has read and thought and
pondered, and then read and thought and pondered again,
till the scattered points of truth which once he saw have
come to find their place and find their meaning in
the great system of truth to which they belong. The
wise man does not carry us away as the prophet does ;

he has not the prophet's direct personal appeal. The teaching that he brings to us cannot be grasped in a day or in a week ; we must put ourselves to school with him ; we must come back to his words again and again, if we want to use the wise man wisely, and to make his wisdom our own. But God sends the wise man, even as He sends the prophet, and we need the one as we need the other. My brothers to be ordained to-day, if God means you to be His wise men, do not baulk His purpose. Do not be shallow when you might be deep ; do not be satisfied to live on mere scraps of truth, and to do everything in your parishes except to read and to think. The whole faith shines with its own light, as parts of it can never do. And do you, my brothers of the laity, listen to the wise men whom the Lord has sent to you. The great enemy of faith to-day is not modern knowledge, but modern ignorance, and God sends you His wise men to deliver you from it. There are thousands—indeed, many millions—in England to-day who know the faith too little even to disbelieve it. God's wise men are within your reach—by their writings, if not by their living voices— and you are bound to listen to them. When, after a life-time of futility and misbelief, with nothing even attempted for God and His kingdom, we plead in excuse that we were without faith, what answer shall we give to the question, "Why were you without it ? I sent you My wise men. Did you attend to what they said ? And if not, why not ?" The most instructed Christians to-day fear nothing— neither science nor historical criticism, nor anything else. They know what can be said against their faith, and they have their answer to it ; they know the far greater volume of what can be said in favour of their faith, and are sure that there is no answer to it. They believe in reason as well as in faith, and open every window to the light. Do you read what they say, even on Sundays ? And, if not, why not ?

We have thought of the prophet and of the wise man ; we pass to the humble scribe. Yes, our Lord sends him too, "Behold, I send unto you scribes." The scribe is the steward, the distributor of the household stores, the man who brings to us the best thoughts of others rather than his own. "Every scribe," says our Lord, "who hath been made a disciple to the kingdom of heaven is like unto a man that is a householder, which bringeth forth out of his treasure things new and old." And, my brothers, I desire specially to point out how really our Lord sends the scribe. How often, and how falsely, are we clergy told that we must all be prophets—that, as God's messengers, we must speak "with authority, and not as the scribes." It cannot be so in all cases ; perhaps it cannot be so in most. But the scribe too has his place. We need the prophet to awaken us, and the wise man to reassure our minds ; but awakened and reassured we need the humble scribe to bring to us our daily bread. "Who then is the faithful and wise steward, which his Lord shall set over His household, to give them their portion of food in due season ? Blessed is that servant whom his Lord, when He cometh, shall find so doing." My brothers of the ministry, let us not grieve overmuch if by God's will we are neither prophets nor wise men. Let us never doubt our calling because, as we preach, we can do little for our people but lay before them the best thoughts of others. "Covet earnestly the best gifts" ; covet them and pray for them ; it may be God's will to grant them, and we might have more if we asked more. "Covet earnestly the best gifts," but be calm and faithful and contented, if you have but the lesser. It is a humble office, I know, just to distribute the stores of the house of God, but does not St. Paul say that "those members of the body which seem to be more feeble are necessary" ? Our Lord never blamed men for being scribes ; He blamed them only for being bad scribes. Let us but see that we are "made," and continue, "disciples to the kingdom of heaven" ; let us see that our storehouse is full—that it has the old as well as the new, and the new as well as the old ; let us see that the bread for our people which we "take hot" for their provision on the day we come forth to go to them does not, like the bread of the Gibeonites, become "dry and mouldy" ; if it does, we shall seem to come from a very "far country," a country none the more attractive because it is so far. See, my brothers, that by continually learning more and more yourselves you give men to drink, as Dr. Arnold said, "out of a running stream, and not out of a stagnant pool." Then, though you may be but scribes, you will be the scribes of Christ, sent and used by Him as really as the prophet and the wise man. And do you, of the laity, never despise such. Do not always demand originality. If the word spoken to you is the Word of God, what more do you require ?

III

One word more. Remember that upon the faithful preaching of the divine Word on the one hand, and upon its faithful acceptance on the other, the continued existence of the Church depends. Christ Himself, no doubt, is the one source of life, and He uses His sacraments as well as His Word to convey that life to us. But, indeed, there is no abiding in Christ which does not involve abiding in His Word, and no possibility of sacramental grace except where that Word is known and that Word obeyed. Oh ! that in the Church of England to-day we thought less of maintaining a system, and more of that divine Word on which the continued life of the Church depends. God guards the Church, while we preach and obey His Word ; if we obey it not, our "house is left unto us," and to our human guardianship, and soon there will "not be left one stone upon another that shall not be thrown down." Do you see ? All through nature it is not life that depends upon organization, but organization that depends upon life. Life forms and maintains the organization that it needs ; the dead body soon falls to dust. So it is with the Church of God. It is the life of the body which formed its organization, and maintains it still to-day. If life departs, all will fall into decay. And, my brothers, it is upon the Word of God preached and obeyed that life depends. This goodly "house of God," the Catholic Church, how did it rise ? It was begotten, like every true member of it, "not of corruptible seed, but of incorruptible, through the Word of God, which liveth and abideth for ever. For all flesh is as grass, and all the glory thereof as the flower of grass." Nothing that is merely human is exempt from the law of change and decay. "The grass withereth, and the flower falleth ; but the Word of the Lord abideth for ever. And this is the Word of good tidings which was preached unto you." And if that be so, then it is only as the clergy preach it, and the whole body believes and obeys it, that the Church of God can stand.

CHRISTIAN CONFIDENCE

THE FIRST SUNDAY OF THE YEAR

"Comfort ye, comfort ye my people, saith your God." —
ISA. xl. 1.

HERE plainly is my commission to-night. All of you, be
your lives what they may, are the people of God ; God
is your God. Before you, as before Israel when these
words were spoken, there is opening a new period of time,
full, to all who live for Him, of splendid possibilities.
And God surely says now, as He said then, "Comfort ye,
comfort ye my people." Encourage them, make them
strong, show them my purpose for them, so that they may
go forward full of confidence in all that I am going to do
for them, and full of determination not by their own fault
to lose one particle of the blessing that I am ready to give.

I

You see then what my commission is. And the way in
which I shall try to perform it is by setting before you the
teaching of that fortieth chapter of Isaiah which was read
to us to-night. Very familiar are many of its verses to those
who worship in a Cathedral Church. Handel has set them
to music, which wonderfully brings out their meaning, and
we have but lately had the pleasure of listening to it.
Again and again to-night, as I quote Isaiah's words, the
music will seem again to be sounding in your ears. But
the words should be far more to us than a reminder of
Handel's music. They should be words, whose meaning

for ourselves we understand, and in whose strength we may
live all through the coming year. For this is characteristic of all God's calls to us to comfort others : He gives,
with the call to comfort, the divine truths by which the
comforting can be done. To comfort is far more than
to sympathize. The best comforter is not the man who
says to the suffering how much he feels for their suffering ;
he is the man who can raise them out of and above the
suffering by showing them how much there is in which to
rejoice. So it is in this noble chapter. I can neither see nor
enable you to see all that there is in it ; but I am sure
that, if I could, there is not one of you who would not
go from this church to-night strong to face the coming
year, and determined that, God helping you, you will not
mar the fulfilment of aught that God intends. The words
were spoken long ago at a great crisis in the history of
God's people Israel. They had been suffering for their
sins by being exiled in a foreign land, and God was about
to restore them to their old home. But the great truths
which the prophet set before them were not truths for
them alone. God's dealings with us, His people, since, and
especially through our Lord Jesus Christ, have only made
us more certain of them. All of them centre round God
Himself, round what He is and what He is ready to do ;
and, whatever may change, God, our God, never changes.
So we shall listen—shall we not ?—to the prophet's
words to-night as spoken to ourselves, and may God fill
them with as much comfort and strength to us as they
brought on the day when first they were spoken !

II

Well ! then, we ask, what does the prophet say ? His
first message is the message which we all need first ; it is
the message of the divine pardon. "Speak ye to the heart
of Jerusalem"—so the words, I think, ought to be translated—"and say unto her, that her time of service is
accomplished, that her iniquity is pardoned ; that she hath

received of the Lord's hand double for all her sin." The prophet's mind, as we soon shall see, is fixed chiefly upon the future, as our minds are to-night, but he begins with the past; he says that God's forgiveness is already granted for it. That is the message which the Church of Christ is sent to carry to the whole world. The message is not only that God will pardon us, but that in a true sense God has pardoned us already. By our Lord Jesus Christ a great sacrifice has been offered for the sins of the whole people of God ; God has accepted it and granted the pardon which it was offered to win. It is true that you and I cannot as individuals share in it, unless we repent and yield ourselves to God. But the pardon has been granted already. It is like a great sum of money paid in for us at the Bank. We must go and claim it, but it is waiting for us already.

Now that is a splendid thought with which to begin the New Year. The moment we repent and ask for pardon, the pardon will be ours. Life perhaps in the past year has seemed a time of hard service ; our work has been a drudgery because we have been forgetting God, and not doing it for Him. Our sins have been weighing us down and shutting out from us the light of God's face ; the troubles that have come to us in the past year have seemed to come as God's judgments upon us, and we seemed to know only too well why they came. But now, if only we will have it so, that past is done with. Our drudgery is accomplished, our iniquity is pardoned ; God counts our sufferings as an ample penance for what we have done. Let the New Year then bring a new beginning ; seek and claim the pardon won for you ; draw a line between the past and the future ; cut your losses and start afresh in the light of God's forgiving love.

Thus far then for the past ; now for the future. What has the prophet to tell us about that ? God tells us this—that in the future He has a splendid purpose for each one of us, and that all His power is pledged to us that we may realize it. Listen ; it is a glorious message. "All flesh is grass, and all the goodliness thereof is as the flower of the field. . . . The grass withereth, the flower fadeth, but the Word of our God shall stand for ever." You see, the prophet recognizes our weakness as fully as we recognize it ourselves; he says that we are like the grass and the flowers, strong and vigorous to-day but perishing to-morrow. If the carrying out of God's purpose depended upon you and me, it never would be carried out. But it does not depend upon us; it depends upon God. "The Word of our God shall stand for ever." If He has said a thing, then He will do it; if He has a great purpose for us, then He will see it through. "Hast thou not known?" says the prophet, "Hast thou not heard? The everlasting God, the Lord, the Creator of the ends of the earth, fainteth not, neither is weary." We ourselves faint; we ourselves grow tired—oh! so quickly. But God never does. God has a purpose for every one of us—yes! a purpose still, in spite of all that we have done to spoil it. And that purpose He never lays aside. He sets it before Himself, and works right on till it is accomplished. As you think to-night of the coming year, think of it in the light of God's purpose for you. Never mind what you want to do with yourselves; think of what God wants to do with you, and of how absolutely certain it is that there is not a thing that He wants to do with you that He is not able to do. Understand that it is God Himself who is going to do it. Listen; "The glory of the Lord shall be revealed, and all flesh shall see it together: for the mouth of the Lord hath spoken it." Listen again; "Behold, the Lord God will come as a Mighty One, and His Arm shall rule for Him." Listen again; "He giveth power to the faint; and to him that hath no might He increaseth strength."

Take this chapter, and read it for yourselves. See how the prophet almost exhausts the power of language to make us understand how great God is. He says that the great sea is to God like the little pool of water we can hold in the hollow of our hands. He says that the mountains are to God like the little weights that we place upon the balances. He says that the nations of the world are

like the drop of water left at the bottom of an empty
bucket. He says that God sits above the circle of the
earth, and all we are like grasshoppers beneath Him. He
says that the great sky is like the top of a tent under
which we dwell. He says that the greatest kings are to
Him like the chaff which the wind blows away. He tells
us to lift our eyes to the starry sky, and remember that
God made every star that we see there, and knows each one
from every other. And why does he say all this? Is it
just to make us feel how insignificant we are? Surely not.
It is to comfort us, to fill us with joy and confidence, because
we know that it is the very God who is so infinitely great
who will be at work for each one of us to carry out His
purpose. Do we say, as Isaiah's people said, that our
"way is hid from the Lord, and" our "judgment is passed
away from" our "God"? Do we say that God no longer
takes account of our lives, or cares to bring them to a
worthy end? The prophet will not hear of such thoughts
of God. The knowledge and wisdom of God are just as
infinite as His power and might; He knows every man and
woman of us as He knows every star. Now that is the
confidence, with which we are going to begin this New
Year. God has a purpose of love in this New Year for
every one of us, and all His infinite power and wisdom are
with us to carry it out. "Faithful is He that calleth you,
who will also do it." God, as St. Paul says, "will fulfil
every desire of goodness and every work of faith with
power." If you and I to-night have any desire for goodness in our heart, if our faith in God is leading us to attempt
any work whatsoever for Him, then we may cast ourselves absolutely upon the power and wisdom of God, and
He will certainly see us through.

God's pardon then, God's purpose and power. There
remains one thing more, and that is God's patience. "He
shall feed His flock like a shepherd, He shall gather the
lambs in His arm, and carry them in His bosom, and shall
gently lead those that give suck." And that surely is the
final encouragement which we all require. Do we not feel

D

sometimes, if we believe in God's great purpose for us, that somehow what God asks of us is too great for us, as we know ourselves to be, and that we for our part can never rise to it ? If we do, it is the remembrance of God's patience that we need. God does desire great things for us, and the great things that He desires for us He can Himself accomplish in us. But, though God desires them, He does not expect them all at once. If we give ourselves to God in this coming year, He will lead us on gradually, as a shepherd leads his flock ; He will know, and allow for our weakness, and bear with our failures ; He will ask of us each day as it comes just what we can do in that day, and He will ask no more. Do you know those noble words of St. Augustine, "God is patient, because He is strong, because He is eternal, because He is God" ? How true that is ! If we are weak, if we have but a little time, and are only human, then we are in a hurry, for we cannot afford to be patient. If we are strong, if we have plenty of time, if we have God Himself with us, then we can be gentle, and can wait. And my brothers, it is just because God is infinitely strong because He has all the time there is, because, as St. Augustine says, He is God, that He can bear with our weakness and failures as no one else could bear with them. Only in this coming year give to God a right intention ; desire with all your heart to do His will, and try to do it. Be ready, when you fail, humbly to begin again. And in spite of all temporary failures, God will bring you to His own desired end.

III

You see then the thoughts, with which we are to begin the coming year. There is God's pardon, there is God's purpose and power, and there is God's patience. It is easy to remember them, since they all begin with the same letter. And now, in conclusion, look at the splendid promise with which the prophet closes the chapter. "They that wait upon the Lord shall renew their strength, they shall mount up with wings as eagles ; they shall run and not be weary ; they shall walk, and not faint." Ah ! we have been trying—have we not ?—to mount up with wings to-night. We have been trying to rise above low thoughts about ourselves, to look at these lives of ours as God looks at them, to see far ahead, as the eagle sees, into all that God desires to make of us. We ought to begin the New Year—rather, let us say, we will begin the New Year—with high hopes, and strong resolutions to be faithful to the highest that we see. But shall we persevere ? —that is the question. We have begun well before, and perhaps after all accomplished but little. How will it be with us in the year that is coming ? My brothers, it will depend upon our waiting on the Lord—upon the trust that we are able to place in Him, and on the continual prayer which will keep that trust and confidence alive. People tell us that we lose our ideals as we grow older. When we are young, we mount up with wings as eagles ; we are full of great ideas as to what we shall do, and what we shall be. We run and are not weary ; we walk and are not faint. But as we grow older, they say, all that dies away ; we come to think as others think, and to do as others do. Do not believe them. It is absolutely false, if only we wait upon God. Be men of faith, be men of prayer, and your ideals will never grow dim ; all through your working-days, you will run and not be weary ; and when you grow old, and can no longer run as once you did, even then, by waiting upon God, you will walk and not faint.

How was it with Him, our Lord, who more than all others, lived the life of waiting upon God ? Wonderful ideas came to Him when He was young—His very temptations show it to us—of what God meant Him to do, of the kingdom of God that He was to establish, and of His own great central place within it. All through His ministry He laboured for what He saw. He gave Himself at times no leisure even to eat ; He ran and was not weary ; ever He did God's will moment by moment, and passed on to the next task laid upon Him. But because He ever waited

upon God and lived in His presence, He never lost the
confidence with which He began ; He went to His death
as certain of God's purpose as when He began His ministry,
and even in the last awful struggle of Gethsemane and
Calvary, He walked and did not faint.   And, my brothers,
if you too will but wait on God—if, come what may in the
New Year, you will but trust Him and never cease to pray
to Him—you too will renew your strength day by day.
What you see now you will never cease to see ; in your
daily duties, you too will run and not be weary ; and even
when the last conflict comes, you will walk and not faint.

THE PAIN OF THE WORLD

SEXAGESIMA

"Unto the woman he said, I will greatly multiply thy
sorrow and thy conception ; in sorrow thou shalt bring
forth children ; and thy desire shall be to thy husband, and
he shall rule over thee. And unto Adam he said, because
thou hast hearkened unto the voice of thy wife, and hast
eaten of the tree, of which I commanded thee, saying,
Thou shalt not eat of it : cursed is the ground for thy
sake ; in toil shalt thou eat of it all the days of thy life."—
GEN. iii 16, 17.

IT was a wonderful chapter that was read to us this morning, wonderful in its knowledge both of human nature and
of human life. It was allegory, no doubt, not history ; the
wisest of the Christian Fathers regarded it much as we
regard it to-day. But, regard it as we may, it is none the
less true. Sin has entered into God's world as this chapter
says that it has ; and the life both of women and of men
is the life which this chapter describes. Indeed evil in
some of its forms does not belong to man alone. As St.
Paul says, "the whole creation groaneth and travaileth in
pain together until now." The sympathy of nature with
man is not, as it has been called, "a pathetic fallacy." It
finds a basis in Scripture and in experience also.

I

But it is not to this thought that I would ask your
attention this morning, but to the view which our faith
leads us to take of the pain and sorrow of the world. All
of us, I suppose, who think at all, have thought about that
problem ; to some it always remains a real and pressing

difficulty. For what are the facts ? On the one hand, there is overflowing evidence of the love of God. The world which He has given to us is a beautiful world ; it seems full of contrivances for the happiness and enrichment of our lives. Human nature itself is fundamentally a noble thing ; the very attention that we pay to our sin and to our suffering shows how unnatural we feel them to be. And yet, on the other hand, there is so much pain and sorrow and failure that it is hard to believe in a God of love. If God be good, we say, why is the world so hard for us and for others ? Why does He not intervene to set it right ?

Observe then how faithful to the facts the Bible is. It does not, like some religious people, merely speak in a soothing way of all being for the best. Nor does it, like some irreligious people, complain or blaspheme because of the existing suffering. On the contrary, from the first it lays its strong grasp upon both sides of the truth. It tells us that the world as God created it was very good ; and that man was made in the image of God to "subdue" the world, and be the lord of the whole. And yet it speaks of us as fallen, and of the world as fallen with us. It says that the ground is cursed for our sake, and that in the sweat of our faces we must eat bread till we return to the ground. What interest this faithfulness to the facts ought to give to us in any explanation that the Bible may have to offer ! If the Bible can "justify the ways of God to man," it will do so with a wide outlook upon those ways themselves.

II

What then, in outline, is the answer which the Bible gives ? It is that the pain and sorrow of the world are neither God's first will nor His last. All that is noble and beautiful in the world without, and in the human soul within, comes from the good God, and reveals His character. If there is much that is otherwise, that is not, in the truest sense, God's will ; largely we have ourselves to thank for it ; and we must work with God that it may pass away. It is not easy to believe this ; but I will try to justify it. Now I suppose that the difficulty presented to our minds arises from our conviction that the world is the expression of the will of God. That is, no doubt, perfectly true ; but it does not follow that God is equally responsible for all that takes place in it. Some things God wills unconditionally ; some things He only wills, if the sins are committed which bring them about. Remember those touching words, in which our Lord lamented over Jerusalem : "O Jerusalem, Jerusalem, which killest the prophets, and stoneth them that are sent unto her ! how often would I have gathered thy children together, even as a hen gathereth her chickens under her wings, and ye would not ! Behold, your house is left unto you desolate." God's will in the highest sense—His antecedent will—was to gather His people under the wings of His divine protection ; if, in a secondary sense, it was His will that Jerusalem should perish, that was because the sin of Jerusalem rendered it necessary.

You see then what I mean by saying that God is not equally responsible for all that takes place. It is we ourselves who are the causes of our own actions, and of all that follows from them. We men have been made in the image of God, and that image is especially seen in our moral freedom. We have, as experience proves, the power of producing results even in the material world by the exercise of our wills. I will to raise my hand, and my hand rises. How that can be, and what is the mysterious link that unites the mental fact of my will with the material fact of the raising of my hand, there is no one who can tell us. But so it is. Just as in creation God "spake and it was done ; He commanded, and it stood fast ;" so, within our tiny sphere of action, we too speak, and it is done ; we command, and it stands fast. Now observe that in all such cases it is we ourselves who are responsible. We are not just secondary causes, as a dynamite bomb is the cause of an explosion ; we are the real causes, with whom the responsibility rests. Argue as we will, we hold ourselves and others responsible—especially others ; we are at peace or remorseful in the one case, we praise or we blame in the other, according as right or wrong has been done. No doubt all the evil might have been avoided if God had denied freedom to us, but then we should not have been men. Outwardly, indeed, we might have looked like men, but inwardly we should have been as really machines as our clocks and our steam engines.

Do you think that the world which would have resulted would have been a better world than this one ? Sin, and the suffering which it brings, might indeed have been absent, but purity and courage and justice and love would have been absent also, for goodness implies moral choice. The brave man is the man who resists the temptation to shrink from danger ; the unselfish man is the man who seeks the good of others when it is entirely open to him to seek only his own. Face the alternatives. Would you rather have this world, even as it is, or a world in which you could never labour or suffer for anyone, and no one could ever labour or suffer for you. In the very nature of things, as far as we can see, either evil must be possible for us, or good, in the true sense, must be impossible. A forced goodness is no goodness ; it is a combination of words that has no meaning. God has chosen the higher and nobler alternative ; He has made us free ; He has made us men. Had He acted otherwise, neither holiness here, nor eternal blessedness hereafter, would be possible for any one of us. That does not mean that the world is abandoned to our folly and our selfishness ; our powers, misuse them as we will, are too small for that. Still God controls the world, and guides it forward to its goal.

> There's a divinity that shapes our ends
> Rough-hew them how we will.

But still we are free ; we do as we will, not always as God wills ; here and now we turn continually the possibility of evil into the reality of it ; and for the result, it is we, and not God, who must bear the blame.

But then can we say that suffering springs altogether from our sin ? There are difficulties in that view, no doubt. Let us see how far we can meet them.

Now it will not be denied that the pain of the world springs very largely from what we ourselves have done. Of all the evils from which you and I suffer to-day, how many would be absent if we had always done the will of God ! How many would be absent, if our forefathers had done it ! How much of our tendency to disease, how much of our weakness both of mind and body, might have been absent if our fathers had done God's will, and passed on to us their strength unimpaired ! Is it not true of many of our lost blessings that, in Jeremiah's words, "Your iniquities have turned away these things, and your sins have witholden good things from you"? Yes, and it is not from our own and our fathers' sins alone that the suffering comes, since for good and for evil the human race is one. For good and for evil the acts that we perform never die ; they go to work in the world, and no one can trace their consequences. The rulers of a country engage in an unjust war, and all its people are impoverished. Nor does the evil stop even then. The impoverished people cannot buy the things that they need ; and those who would have supplied their need are thrown out of employment.

Does it seem to us unjust that this should be so ? If so, let us remember that we receive good even more than evil by the closeness of our union with our fellow-men, and that we cannot enjoy the one without being exposed to the other. Let us remember also that if we could injure no one but ourselves, one of our best and strongest motives for goodness would be taken away. But think of it as we will, vast numbers of the evils from which we suffer spring directly from our personal and from our corporate sins, and it is we and not God who must bear the blame.

But then it will be said that this is far from covering the ground ; there is much pain in the world which cannot be due to our sin. The lightning strikes a tree, and a man is crushed as it falls. A fog comes up on a winter night and

obscures the signals, and in a moment one train is hurled
into another. The lightning and the fog lies at God's
door ; what can they have to do with the sin of man ?   My
brothers, I believe that even here there is the closest
connection.   We need not suppose that the laws of the world
were changed when we first fell into sin.   But an imperfect
world is the best training-place for imperfect men and
women ; and the world is what it is because God knew that
we should be what we are.

> "Now by the verdure on thy thousand hills,
> Beloved England, doth the earth appear
> Quite good enough for men to overbear
> The will of God in, with rebellious wills."

But there is more than this.   The imperfections of the
world are meant to be corrected by our own activity.   God
made man to become the lord of the world ; not only to
replenish the earth, but to subdue it.   The world is not
just a picture to be gazed at, and enjoyed ; it is a workshop
full of mighty forces that we must learn to understand and
control.   The command to subdue the world is a call to
the acquisition and use of scientific knowledge.   When
in George Eliot's novel *Middlemarch* the great doctor
Lydgate, with his divine vocation to become a man of
science, sacrificed his vocation in order to make money and
keep an extravagant wife in luxury, he sinned against
humanity and against God.   We are made to seek for
truth, even as we are made to seek for goodness and for
beauty ; and if from the first we had studied the world and
its forces as we ought to have studied them, there might be
no single force in our world to-day that we could not harness
for our use.   How wonderfully we have learnt to control
these forces even now !   The same electricity, which
undirected blasts our trees, brought under control we use
to light our streets ; the same laws and forces by which the
fog rises and the volcano breaks out, we can employ, when
we know and can control them, to drive the wheels of our
mills and steam-engines.   And if this be so in spite of our
past indolence, what might not our powers have been, had

we observed and laboured as we should ? May we not then believe that those mighty forces which now seem so destructive are an example not of God's carelessness of us but of God's generosity to us ? God meant them unto good.

III

My brothers, I have not solved the mystery ; a mystery it must remain. But I have tried to show you that, when the book of Genesis says that the ground is cursed for our sakes, it says what is strictly true. Will you say that, be this as it may, pain is here, and that, whatever its cause, it remains equally hard to bear ? I do not think so. Is it not much to find the clouds passing away from our Father's character ? Is it not much to find in the pain and sorrow of the world, not a reason for complaint, but a motive for repentance ? But there is more than this. Does not the true view open to us a vision of the grandest hope ? If the evil directly came from God, if it were in the fullest sense His will, what could we do but fold our hands, and endure ? But if it comes from ourselves, if in the deepest sense it is not God's will, if He meant and means something very different, may we not hope, in Him and with Him, at last to be free from it ?

Well, if we would do so, we must begin by dealing with ourselves. The evil of the world is a mighty river, but it is daily fed by the little rills which rise within our own breasts ; and, if we cannot at once dam the mighty river, we can choke the little streams that go to swell it. Every time that you or I resist a temptation, or help another to resist it, we do something to lessen the pain of the world. In the end the world will be a little brighter than it would have been if we had not been here.

Can we not learn this from the example of our Lord Himself ? He, if any one, knew what the pain was, for He above all others was a man of sorrows and acquainted with grief. How did He regard it ? How did He deal with it ? He passed through the world, never complaining of

sorrow, never impatient under it, never even surprised at
it ; but, when faith was present, never failing to relieve it.
And yet, behind all the pain, He saw ever the sin from which
it sprang, and made it the purpose of His life and of His
Death, of His Resurrection and of His abiding activity, to
deal with that. And if since His coming the burden of
pain has been at all lightened for us—if, as His Kingdom
spreads, "the habitations of cruelty" a little give place to
the peace and joy of the Christian life, why is it ? It is not
because of the cures that He wrought while He was here ;
it is not that He changed the laws of the world, and made
wilful sin less fruitful in suffering. It is because with
Him there came into the world a new power, through
which our wills can be renewed, so that we cease to give
pain, because we have ceased to sin.

SIMON THE PHARISEE

THE SECOND SUNDAY IN LENT

"And Jesus answering said unto him, Simon, I have
somewhat to say unto thee. And he saith, Master, say
on. A certain lender had two debtors : the one owed five
hundred pence, and the other fifty. When they had not
wherewith to pay, he forgave them both."—LUKE vii.
40-42.

IT is a wonderful story from which these words are taken ;
perhaps there is no other in the Gospels on which so many
Lenten sermons have been preached. But we will not
think chiefly to-day of the woman who was a sinner, but
of Simon the Pharisee, in whose house her acts of love
took place. It was to him that the Lord chiefly spoke, and
it is with him perhaps that we have more in common.
"Simon, I have somewhat to say unto thee." "Master,
say on." Perhaps in speaking to Simon, the Lord will
speak to us.

I

We look then at Simon himself. Our Lord at first made
no attack upon the Pharisees. That tremendous denuncia-
tion, "Woe unto you, scribes and Pharisees, hypocrites",
was the fruit of later experience. His message was to the
whole people of God ; and He appealed to the Pharisees as
He appealed to the rest. Nor apparently were the Pharisees at first hostile to the Lord. "Rabbi," said the Pharisee Nicodemus, "we know that Thou art a Teacher come
from God." With Simon the case is similar. He asks the
Lord to a meal in his house, and is ready to listen to what
He has to say. But that is as far as he goes. He has no

sense of personal need ; he is satisfied with his religion and with himself ; and so the Lord's gospel of the kingdom, the Lord's offer of forgiveness that we may be ready to enter it, finds but little response in Simon's heart. Though he is not hostile, he is far from cordial. The customary bath for the feet, the kiss of welcome, are absent ; there is no perfumed oil for the head of his guest. Is it not enough that this untaught Galilean should be invited to sit at Simon's table ? Indeed, Simon does not understand the Lord's outlook, and has a poor opinion of His powers. If the Lord permits the touch of a woman of evil fame, it must be that He lacks the prophet's insight into character.

Now how does the Lord deal with Simon ? He feels his discourtesy, and tells Simon that He feels it. But with a gentle Socratic irony he suggests that the divine forgiveness which he comes to bestow is not worth to such a man as Simon what it is worth to a woman of the town ; it is only to be expected that he will not be equally grateful. "To whom little is forgiven, the same loveth little." And then He turns to the woman and bestows the fulness of His blessing, "Thy sins are forgiven, go in peace."

II

My brothers, let us think of this. Simon is no uncommon character. We often meet him ; especially perhaps when, as St. James puts it, we look at our natural faces in the glass. Would that William Law were here to describe him in his own inimitable way ! Our modern Simon is quite a religious person ; religion indeed is his chief interest. And Simon is not narrow minded. He likes to hear about new views. And, if a new teacher has something fresh to say, Simon is quite ready to ask him to dinner. Moreover, our modern Simon is some sort of a Christian. He thinks highly of our Lord's moral teaching—"Master, say on." He is a regular communicant ; in the Blessed Sacrament he often receives our Lord under his roof. But how about Simon's love ? Well ! Simon is an Englishman, and

undemonstrative ; the warmer language of Christian devotion, the perfume and the kiss, do not appeal to him ; and,
as to outward demonstrations of respect when he receives
the Lord, Simon has always disliked ceremonial. Simon,
he would have us know, believes in a practical Christianity ;
and the one way of showing love to Christ is to live a good
life.

How then does Simon live it ? If he believes in deeds,
not in words, to what particular deeds of his does he refer ?
What exactly is it that Simon does which he would not do for
one reason or another, if he were not a Christian ? What
exactly are the sacrifices which he makes to show his
gratitude to the Lord Christ ? Perhaps we are becoming
too particular in our enquiries ; what he does, Simon
says, is his own business and not ours. Now it is at this
point that the Lord intervenes with a suggestion. If
Simon is not a great lover, it is because he is not a great
penitent ; and how can we expect him to be that ? Simon
was always "virtuously given" ; he was the pride and joy
of his parents ; he took all the prizes at school ; and he has
lived the rest of his life according to this beginning. Thus
to-day he owes no man anything, and God very little.
If he ever had any debt to be forgiven, it was but a five
shilling matter. So now we understand. The reason why
Simon loves God and man so little is that he is such an
exceedingly good man.

Well ! it is all very logical ; but we have reached a somewhat Gilbertian conclusion. Is there not a catch somewhere ? Sin and forgiveness are rather deep matters, and
perhaps our simple Simon does not fully understand them.
How did the Lord speak of them, not to Simon, but to
those who had left all to follow him ?

The kingdom of heaven is "likened unto a certain king,
which would make a reckoning with his servants." A king
and his servants—let us consider this relation ; we are all
forgetting it to-day. To whom does the world belong ?
Who was it who made it ? And to whom do we and our
fellow-Simons belong ? Who made us ? How comes it

that we are here to-day? And how do we stand to God in view of all this? Whether or no we live well in a moral and religious sense, we certainly live well in another. The food and raiment that we consume, the labour and service that we are able to claim from others, are very considerable; what right have we to all these things? Certainly they are not our own. Now to that question there is but one satisfying answer. We are God's servants. He has placed us where we are, that we may labour for Him, and forward the accomplishment of His purposes. If we are living to do God service, it is but right that we should take what we require that we may perform the service that He asks of us. If we are Christ's as Christ is God's—so St. Paul says—all things are ours; if we are Christ's, but not otherwise. If we are not the servants of the heavenly king, what claim can we make upon His property?

So, you see, the king must make a reckoning. How then about Simon? Is Simon worth—we will not say "his salt," for salt is cheap—but all those valuable products of nature and industry which he is continually consuming? We must cast up his ledger; we must balance what he has received against what he has done. If the balance is on the credit side, that will be Simon's merit; if on the debit side, that will be Simon's debt to God and man. Is it a five shilling matter? What says the Lord? When the king "had begun to reckon, one was brought unto him which owed him ten thousand talents." What right then has Simon to all that he enjoys? What right to "his wife, and children, and all that he has?" Obviously, Simon must be sold up; he and his family must be sent to the slave-market, and his goods knocked down to the highest bidder; he will hardly pay a penny in the pound even then. And if God forgives Simon, and bears with him in hope of better things, what will Simon's debt to God be for that? "Seest thou this woman?" One of you owes five hundred pence and one fifty. Be it so. But which of you is it that owes the one, and which of you is it that

owes the other ? Are you quite sure, Simon ? Think of
what you have had, and of what she has had—not only
of material things, but of nature, and education, and advan-
tages of every kind. Bankrupt both, no doubt ; but are
you sure that you have not failed for more than she has ?
Which of you then ought to love God most ? Do you understand what forgiveness means ? Is it a trifle light as air,
a thing wanting in practical reality ? Do you not see that
those blessings which you have forfeited, but which are
left to you still, are themselves the present and probationary forgiveness that you enjoy ? "It is of the Lord's
mercies that we are not consumed, and because His com-
passions fail not." Your liberty, your wife, your children,
all that you have, are themselves your forgiveness. Forgiveness manages your household for you, that you may
be free for other things. Forgiveness pours out your tea
in the afternoon. Forgiveness comes gaily home for the
holidays. Forgiveness arrives by post from the Bank of
England on dividend day. Is forgiveness an airy nothing,
or as "solid comfort" as anything in the world ?

III

Well ! Simon, what about it ? When that poor woman
came in, and knelt at the Lord's feet ; and the tears came
in a flood before she could control them, and she wiped
them away with her hair, what did you think of it all ?
Very unpleasant it was—was it not ?—very awkward for
everybody ? What a thing to happen in your dining-room !
If you had only known what your invitation to Jesus
might bring in its train ! That is the worst of bringing
Jesus into our lives ; the most disreputable people are sure
to come in after Him. But ought not you to have been
kneeling by her ? And, my brothers, what of ourselves ?
How little any of us grasp the situation ! Do we not all
need to pray our Lenten Collect ? "Create and make in
us new and contrite hearts, that we worthily lamenting
our sins and acknowledging our wickedness, may obtain

E

of Thee, the God of all mercy, perfect remission and forgiveness." Forgiveness, you see, is twofold. There is the present and probationary forgiveness that is ours already, the continuance of our blessings and opportunities, in spite of all that we have done to forfeit them ; and there is that perfect remission and forgiveness which brings union with God and eternal life. But the second will only be ours when we are real penitents.

the.
hope c.
for that :
hundre.
is it th.

SERMON VIII

SONSHIP TO GOD

THE FOURTH SUNDAY IN LENT

"Son, thou art ever with me, and all that is mine is
thine. But it was meet to make merry and be glad : for
this thy brother was dead, and is alive again ; and was lost,
and is found."—LUKE xv. 31, 32.

THESE words surely spring from the heart of our Lord's
experience. He Himself was "ever with" the Father ; He
Himself says that all that the Father has is His : He
Himself came to give life to the "dead," to seek and to save
that which was "lost." And what He teaches is that as
He was, so we are to be in this world ; we too are to be sons
of God, heirs of God, "merry and glad" for nothing so much
as for the salvation of His children.

I

You see then the way in which we shall consider these
words this morning. We shall regard them as a revelation
of that life of sonship, which God intends for us all. The
parables of our Lord generally have but one main lesson ;
we should begin by ascertaining what it is, and laying
hold of it. But there are parables, which seem to be
allegories as well as parables, and in which almost every
word is significant ; in these, when we have grasped the main
lesson, we should proceed to grasp the minor ones also.
Now the parable of the prodigal son is a case in point. The
main lesson, of course, is the Father's love for the lost child,
the fulness and freedom of his forgiveness. But there are
other lessons in the parable than that ; and we must not

let the splendour of the main one blind us to their importance. The father in the parable had two sons, and we
should learn from the elder as well as from the younger.

Now the pathos of the story lies largely in this, that
neither the one son nor the other returned his father's love.
The younger son might be a wastrel, and the elder a well-
conducted and hard-working man ; but, as far as love for
their father was concerned, there was but little to choose
between them. Listen to the elder as he speaks to his
father. "Lo, these many years do I serve thee, and never
transgressed a commandment of thine ; and yet thou never
gavest me a kid, that I might make merry with my friends."
Neither he nor his brother cared to be with his father. To
each enjoyment meant to leave his father, and make merry
with his chosen associates ; the father was simply the
banker to provide the means for doing so. No doubt the
elder brother's friends were persons of the highest respect-
ability ; but they were just as much in his heart the successful rivals of his father as the evil-livers with whom his
brother consorted. This elder son was in fact as little a
son as he was a brother ; and the purpose of the father's
words was to recall him to true sonship as well as to true
brotherhood. "Son, thou art ever with me, and all that
is mine is thine." Is the common life, the common inheritance, nothing to you ? "It was meet to make merry and
be glad : for this thy brother was dead, and is alive again ;
and was lost, and is found."

II

My brothers, these are wonderful words ; perhaps we
greatly need them. God's prodigal sons are seldom with
us in the house of God ; would that they were with us
more often, that they might learn of their Father's love !
But God's elder sons, who have served Him "these many
years", and yet have never learnt to be sons to Him, are
with us Sunday by Sunday. How they also need to learn
His love, and what that love asks of them ! Now our Lord,

the true and perfect Son, teaches us what the son's life means; and how he should feel and act towards God, towards his brothers, and towards the world. Let us listen and learn.

There is God first, God who is our Father. What is the spirit of the Son towards Him? "Son, thou art ever with Me." To be a son to God is just that; it is to be ever with our Father, and to find our highest satisfaction in being there. Union with God is the all-embracing blessing; to possess it is to possess the thing which is best worth having. How our Lord cared for it, both for Himself and for us! "The Son abideth in the house for ever." "This is life eternal, that they should know Thee, the only true God." Jesus never looked upon union with the Father just as a means to something beyond itself; it might be nearer to the truth to say that all else was a means to that.

Now, if we would be indeed the sons of God, that should be our spirit also. We should not seek after God just for the sake of other things, however high and noble they may be; we should seek Him for Himself. It is true that union with God is necessary for all life that is worthy of the name; separated from Him we can neither be our true selves, nor effect anything that is worth effecting in the world around us. But if we wish to find God, we should seek Him for Himself. Perhaps a simple illustration will make this clear. It is true that a happy marriage is a great help to the living of a pure and holy life; it is also a great help to a man's work in the world. But we should not be likely to win our wives if we sought them simply in view of these things. We seek and win our wives because we love them, because to be "ever with" them is the very thing that we most desire.

Now is God less worth winning for His own sake than our wives for theirs? Yet how we forget this! Listen to the pious Englishman as he stands up for religion. "Depend upon it," he says, "if religion disappears, morality will disappear with it." Most true, no doubt; but we

should not seek for union with the eternal God in order to
lighten the labours of the police. Morality is a valuable
by-product of religion, not the end which we have in view.
The end which we have in view is union with God for His
own sake. Jesus Christ taught us to be pure in heart, that
we might see God ; not to see God that we might be pure
in heart ; and the true son will always put his father
first.

Secondly, how will the true son act towards his brothers ?
Ever in his ears there will ring the Father's words "This
thy brother " ; and ever he will love and serve them for
his Father's sake. How was it with the Lord Himself ?
His love to men did not rest upon their natural attractiveness ; we were a weight upon His soul. "O faithless and
perverse generation !" the Lord said ; "how long shall I
be with you ? How long shall I suffer you ?" He loved
men and served men from His sense of their infinite value
in the Father's eyes. That was why He went after the
publicans and sinners. The elder brothers of His day
blamed Him for doing so. They did not understand that
we can love those whom we do not like, since love is a
matter of self-sacrificing will, and liking but the natural
consequence of attractiveness to ourselves. Thus they
supposed that our Lord consorted with the outcasts because
it was their society that He found most congenial. And
what was His reply ? Simply that a man was to God as a
lost soul, a lost sheep, whom he could not afford to lose,
a lost son whose empty chair he could not bear to see ; and
that the sinner who had wandered away from God often did
what he did because he saw no other course open to him.
Jesus was so full of pity and hope in dealing with publicans
and sinners, and the Pharisees so hard and hopeless,
because Jesus understood them and the Pharisees did not.
"How infamous," said the Pharisee, "for men to live by
collecting taxes for the Roman oppressor ! How infamous
for women to live by their shame !" No doubt ; but the
Pharisees did not see that neither the men nor the women
always lived as they did for the love of so living. Many

lived as they did, because, like the prodigal, they had spent all, and could find no other way of living at all. When the Lord said that "the prodigal joined himself to the citizen of the far country, and was sent into his fields to feed swine," it was of the dirty work of the publicans that he was thinking. When he said of the prodigal, "He would fain have been filled with the husks that the swine did eat : and no man gave unto him," he told us the reason why men are willing to live as the beasts. It is because they think that the life of a man is no longer for them.

But then we shall never understand all this, until we love the Father, and our Father's home. Always it is the true son who is the true brother. When the elder son in the parable was angered by the welcome of the prodigal, when he said not "this my brother," but "this thy son, which hath devoured thy living with harlots," he showed that he loved neither his father nor his home. The truth was that he half envied his brother ; and thought that his brother had been happier in his life of sin than he himself had been in his life of service. Thus, when the father gave to the prodigal so great a welcome, when he sent for the town dancers and the town band, he felt that it only increased the unmerited enjoyment which his brother had had already. And from what does our own hardness often spring but from the same suspicion ? We serve God without loving Him, and find that our lives are dull. We think that the sinners are enjoying all that we are missing, living a larger and fuller life than ours ; and so that for God to welcome them back is to allow them to have it both ways. Poor elder brothers ! And we shall never be any better until we know our Father and love our home, and so find His service perfect freedom. Then we shall no more envy sinners. We shall know that what the world calls seeing life is really undergoing death, that all who are separated from God are before very long starving and miserable. We too shall love them then, even though we may not like them, and do all we can for them from love to God and pity for them.

God then, and men, and finally the world. How does the true son regard that ? "Son, thou art ever with me, and all that is mine is thine." Yes, that is true ; the son is the heir. If we are God's sons, then all that is God's is also ours ; ours now and ours for ever. Do these words seem to you unreal and meaningless ? Then think what possession means. Possession, ownership—it is not a matter of sealing-wax and parchments ; we possess that, and that only, by which we enrich our personal life, and forward our work in the world. What do we mean when we say that "the earth is the Lord's, and the fulness thereof ?" Do we mean that God owns it as we own money in the bank ; that He can do what He wills with His own, and annihilate the world as easily as create it ? Poor indeed would such possession be. Or do we mean that all that God has made is known and appreciated by Him, that it forms (if we may so say) part of the wealth of His personal life, that He uses its resources for the fulfilment of His purposes, and will find a place for everything when His purpose is attained ? Possession lies not in the power to hoard or to destroy ; it lies in appreciation, enrichment, and love.

And so it is with ourselves. The true owner of the world is the man whom the world is serving, the man who can take the world to his heart, as St. Francis did, and find himself in a living relation to his brother the sun, and the beauty of earth and sea and sky, as well as to the human brothers and sisters by whom he is surrounded, and to the Father from whom all good things come. Who was the true possessor of the Holy Land when the Lord was there ? Tiberius Cæsar, who had never seen it, or the Lord Himself who loved the beauty of its flowers and saw the deepest laws of God's kingdom written large upon its life ? Who owns the world today—the millionaire, who, in his devotion to money has lost all power to enjoy it, or the humble Christian man who loves it as his Father's handiwork, sees always the love and wisdom of God written upon it, and finds it all serving him, as he does his Father's will ? "Thou never gavest me a kid." Poor elder brother ! What did he want with a dead kid away from his father, when he had the whole estate to use and enjoy with him ? That is the Christian way. Seek nothing apart from God, and you will find that you have everything with Him. "All things are yours ; whether Paul, or Apollos, or Cephas, or the world, or life or death, or things present, or things to come : all are yours, and ye are Christ's and Christ is God's.''

THE BURNING BUSH

Passion Sunday

"And the angel of the Lord appeared to him in a flame of fire out of the midst of a bush : and he looked, and behold, the bush burned with fire, and the bush was not consumed."
—Ex. iii. 2.

It is, I think, with profound insight that the Church has chosen the lections for to-day. The burning bush is a picture of our Lord Himself, with the fire of His Godhead burning within and yet leaving his Manhood unconsumed. And, though it is true that in the Passion of the Lord His glory is to the outward eye more than ever veiled, to those who understand His revelation it is then peculiarly manifest. So, like Moses in the Bible story, we will turn aside now, and see this great sight, why the bush is not burnt. Perhaps out of the midst of the fire God will speak to us also.

I

We look then first at the Bible story. It is the story of a theophany, of a manifestation of God to one called to do a great work for Him. "The angel of the Lord" is a figure which frequently appears in the earlier parts of the Bible. *The* angel of the Lord is not the same as *an* angel of the Lord. The angel of the Lord is God as manifested to men ; He is identified practically with God Himself. So it is here, when the angel of the Lord speaks : "I am the God of thy father, the God of Abraham, the God of Isaac, and the God of Jacob" ; and our Lord, when he refers to the passage, appears to interpret it in the same sense.

Now there are two points which we should here notice. The first is that, though a new revelation is being made, it

is not a new God who is being revealed. God speaks as
the God of His servants of old, as One who is bound to
them by the promise made to them, and who is about
to fulfil those promises. The second is that the revelation
is a practical revelation ; it will come not so much by what
God says as by what He will do. The God who speaks is
a redeeming God. He has heard the cry of His people ; He
knows their sorrows ; and He has come down to deliver
them from the Egyptians, and to lead them to a land of
their own. Moreover, it is here that the importance of
the name of God seems to lie, that name of Yah-weh, or
Jehovah, which Moses is to give as God's name to the people
of Israel. Scholars are not all agreed as to the meaning
of the name, as the margin of the R.V. will show you.
But the true meaning is probably not "I am that I am",
but "I will be that I will be" ; and it thus speaks to us not
of God's eternal Being as distinct from all that He has
made, but of His continual revelation of Himself to us by
all that He does. Who and what is God ? Ah ! there is
no one who can tell us that. Here we but touch the hem
of His garment. But his name to us is "wait and see," for
"He will be that He will be." To the world at large, to
His Church on earth, to every one who comes to trust
under the shadow of His wings He will be that He will be ;
and, as we live for him, we shall come to understand Him.

So the saints ever tell us. We cannot by searching find
out God. He must reveal Himself, and call us by our names.
But if, when He calls, we answer, and are ready to obey,
God will reveal Himself by what He does for us ; and at
last we shall see Him as He is.

II

We see then the profound meaning of this old-world
story ; let us turn now to that to which it points. Is it a
mere pious fancy which sees our Lord foreshadowed in
the burning bush ? Here perhaps we shall not all give
the same answer. But the early Fathers find in the Angel

of the Lord our Lord Himself ; and, when St. Paul speaks of the spiritual rock which followed God's people in the wilderness, it is not unlikely that he does the same.

But let us judge for ourselves. What was our Lord to the outward eye ? He was a carpenter of Nazareth, a despised town of the half-heathen Galilee, "the back of the wilderness" to the Jews of His day. He grew, like the desert-scrub which Moses saw, as "a root out of a dry ground." He had no form nor comeliness ; and, when men saw Him, there was no beauty that they should desire Him. He was despised, and rejected of men ; a man of sorrows, and acquainted with grief. And yet, as we look at Him, the bush burns with fire. In that strange carpenter of Nazareth there shines out the divine power, the divine wisdom, the divine authority, the divine holiness, the divine love. "Whence hath this man this wisdom and these mighty works"? "What is this ? A new teaching ! With authority he commandeth the unclean spirits, and they obey Him." "Which of you convinceth Me of sin ?" "The Son of Man came to seek and to save that which was lost." So men turn aside in their thousands to see this great sight ; and when He speaks, they know that they must listen ; and when He calls, they know that they must obey. Who then is He ? Is He just an angel, or messenger of God, like the prophets before Him ? Or is He the angel of God, one with God Himself ? Listen to what He says. "All things have been delivered unto Me of My Father ; and no one knoweth who the Son is save the Father ; and who the Father is save the Son, and he to whomsoever the Son willeth to reveal him." "He that hath seen me hath seen the Father. I am in the Father and the Father in me." "I and the Father are one."

But what God is it who is being revealed ? Is it a God unknown before ? So some to-day would have us believe. They would have us scrap the O.T. The world, they think, does not reveal God, or human history either ; we must find God in Christ, and nowhere else. But that is not what the Lord Himself said. The Father of whom

He spoke was the Father who makes His sun to shine upon
the evil and on the good, who feeds the birds, and clothes
the flowers with beauty. He said that to Himself Moses
has borne witness before He came, and that Abraham had
rejoiced to look forward to His day. He came not to
destroy, but to fill to the full the revelation that had been
given before Him. And what was the revelation that He
brought ? It was a practical revelation, a revelation not
in word only, but in power. He said, as the Baptist had
said, that the kingdom of God was at hand ; but unlike
the Baptist, He brought its blessings with Him. His
miracles were the first drops of the promised torrent of
blessing. "The blind receive their sight, and the lame
walk, the lepers are cleansed, and the deaf hear, and the
dead are raised up, and the poor have good tidings preached
to them." You see how practical the revelation was. It
was not only that never man spake like this man, but that
never man did like this man. The Lord was true man still ;
though the bush burns with fire, the bush is not consumed.
But in the Lord, the image of God, we see God Himself
shining out in action for us all. So it was in the Passion and
the Resurrection, as our second lesson reminds us. The
Lord came indeed to minister, but not to minister alone.
He came to give His life a ransom for many, to win for us
our true lives back ; to be mocked and scourged and
crucified, and rise again to give us the salvation He has
won. Thus, too, we are to see the glory of God in the face
of Jesus Christ—God in Christ taking our burden upon
Himself, yielding Himself up to the worst that we can do
to Him, overcoming evil with good, showing us as in a
picture what our sins mean to Him, bearing them with
infinite patience that He may bear them away, overcoming
them that we in Christ may overcome them with Him.

III

My brothers, on Passion Sunday could the Church give
us a better lesson than this ? God may have a work yet for

each one of us to do for Him, but we cannot do it before we know His Name.   We must turn aside first to see this great sight, remembering that the place whereon we stand is holy ground.   God has come down to us that He may redeem us, and at the Cross we see Him most clearly.   Can we trust that revelation and yield ourselves to live by it ? "Which of you convicteth me of sin ?   If I say truth, why do ye not believe me ?"   Words without deeds we may disbelieve ; facts without words we may misunderstand. But when we have words and deeds, the words explaining the deeds, and the deeds proving the words to be true, we have all the aids to faith which God Himself can give us. Only, even as we believe, let us remember that the name of God is "I will be that I will be." That, He says, is "His name for ever, and His memorial unto all generations." And that name means for us all two things.   It means first, as St. Paul seems to say, that not only love, but faith and hope abide.   We can never come to the end of the knowledge of God.   Always we shall find

> some knowledge at each pause,
> Or some new thing to know.

It means, secondly, that just because it is God who must reveal Himself to us, we shall never have the knowledge of God, unless we obey His calls to service, as Moses did, and live close enough to Him for the revelation to be possible.

THE GARDEN OF GETHSEMANE

PALM SUNDAY

"O My Father, if this cannot pass away, except I drink it, Thy will be done."—MATT. xxvi. 42.

THERE are two very different ways in which we may say, "Thy will be done." We may say it humbly indeed, but hopelessly ; and, when things are at their worst, that is generally our way of saying it. But there is another, and a better way. We may say it, as those who deliberately accept suffering for themselves, because they discern more or less clearly a great purpose of God which by their suffering is being fulfilled ; and so fix their minds upon the fulfilment of that purpose rather than upon the suffering which for them it involves. That surely was the Lord's way. He had no love of suffering ; He would have escaped the Cross, had it been possible rightly to do so. But rather than that God's great purpose for the world should fail of its fulfilment, He would have endured it a thousand times.

I

We have come once more to Holy Week, the week of the Lord's passion and of the Lord's victory. "The hour is come, that the Son of Man should be glorified." That is the way in which the Lord looked at it, and the way in which we should look at it ourselves. But Jesus was a man ; none the less a man because He was God in Manhood ; and in His life here He had the limitations which manhood brings. He had to walk by faith, not by sight. The present was to him, if not more certain than the future, more vivid, and more strongly felt. Thus we should not explain away either the scene in Gethsemane or the language used by the Evangelists concerning it. We should speak of it with caution, as of a mystery too great for our full understanding ; but we should accept it just as it stands.

Now the Lord, we read, was "greatly amazed, and sore troubled." There was an abyss opening before Him which was, at the time, beyond His fathoming. He knew, as we know when things are at their hardest, so much and no more. His mind was not, it seems, at first, clear about the will of God for Him. Still less, I think, did He foresee the future in any detail. He knew that beyond the suffering and defeat lay victory and the power to bless, but not, I think, the form which the victory would take. He saw, no doubt, that He would rise again, but that language seems more definite than it is because we read into it our own knowledge of what afterwards took place. All the evidence, I think, suggests that our Lord drew His knowledge of the future from what the Old Testament had revealed about it ; we cannot certainly ascribe to Him a greater knowledge than that. What He had in mind was that wonderful picture of God's suffering Servant which was read to us in our first lesson this morning, and that other picture so very like it, which is found in the twenty-second Psalm ; and both the one and the other go into far greater detail about the suffering than about the glory to which it leads. Let us try then to blend these two pictures into a consistent whole, and see whether the Agony in the Garden does not become a little clearer to us.

II

What then is the experience which these pictures describe ? It is the experience of One who is the Servant or Slave of God. God has a great purpose for the world, and the Servant is the One destined to accomplish it. God, the Psalmist says, took Him out of the womb ; the purpose rests upon Him from the first ; and, if He fails or is overcome, the purpose of God will fail with Him.

But the experience of this Servant of God is far from what might have been expected; it is no wonder that many are "astonied" at Him. How unimpressive at first sight He seems to be ! He is "a worm, and no man." He grows like a desert shrub, a root out of a dry ground ; there is no majesty in His bearing, no beauty in His face. He is despised and rejected by those to whom He goes, a man of sorrows and acquainted with grief. Worse still, He bears the bitter hatred of His people. They compass Him about like savage wild beasts ; they strip Him of His very garments ; they threaten Him with death, unjustly condemn Him, and lead Him as a lamb to the slaughter. But there is worse even than this. In the days of old, as the Psalmist says, God heard the prayer of His servants, and delivered them, when they cried to Him ; but with the Servant that seems not to be so. God seems "far from helping" Him ; He cries, but there is no answer. His enemies, only too naturally, see in His sufferings the judgment of God ; they esteem Him stricken, smitten of God, and afflicted ; and that is almost more than He can bear. That is one side of the picture, and how closely it corresponds to our Lord's experience we may all see for ourselves. St. Paul tells us how the Jews of his day felt what he calls the offence of the Cross. It was a great stumbling-block to them that the great Messiah, the very centre of God's purpose, should reach his position by the way of the Cross. But, if it was so great a stumbling-block to them, was it not perhaps a mystery to the Lord Himself? Can we wonder that on the Cross He, like the Psalmist, asked God why? What was it according to the Epistle to the Hebrews which made the faith of Abraham so great ? It was not just that he was ready to sacrifice his son, but that upon the life of that son the fulfilment of God's promise depended. So surely it was with the Lord. On the Lord, the Christ of God, the hope of the world was resting. If He died with His work undone, how should God's promise be fulfilled ?

F

And now let us look at the other side of the picture, as it must surely have formed itself in the mind of the Lord. It is the picture of one who is suffering indeed, but suffering for no sin of His own. In some mysterious way which the prophet does not explain, He is bearing the griefs of His people, and carrying their sorrows. He is pierced because of their transgressions, crushed because of their iniquities. "All we like sheep have gone astray ; we have turned every one to his own way ; and the Lord hath laid on Him the iniquity of us all." He is like the sin-offering of the old Mosaic law ; He is bearing the burden of human sin, that by His sacrifice he may bear it away. And so, because the sin is not His own, from out of the deep of suffering, humiliation, and death, in some unimaginable way He will rise. God, as the Psalmist says, will show that He has not despised or abhorred the affliction of His servant, nor hid His face from Him. As many were astonied at the greatness of His suffering, so He will "startle many nations" by the wonder of His deliverance. In the great days yet to come, the Servant of God will see His seed, and prolong His days, and the purpose of God will prosper in His hand. To the childless Servant there will be given a vast family to bear His name ; the days which seemed to be brought to an untimely close will be prolonged beyond the suffering and the seeming death ; that great purpose of God which He came to serve will, in His hands, go triumphantly forward. He will reveal the name and character of God to His human brothers, and by His teaching and influence make them righteous like Himself. He will see of the travail of His soul and be satisfied ; for all the ends of the earth shall remember and turn unto the Lord ; and all the kindreds of the nations shall worship before Him.

III

We see then the pictures which the Lord's words suggest to have been in His mind ; and, as we study them, and blend the features of the one with the features of the other, we can see, I think, both how the Lord could pray that, if it were possible, the cup might pass away, and yet, as His mind grew clearer with His prayer, be fully prepared to drink it. For the twenty-second Psalm, though it recalls so many features of the Passion, says not a word of death ; at the last moment deliverance seems to come ; and, though Isaiah's prophecy does speak of death, it speaks also of the Servant as prolonging His days. In the old story of the sacrifice of Isaac, when Abraham's will had been fully surrendered, the actual sacrifice was no longer required ; and might it not have proved so with the Lord Himself ?

I do not see any signs in the Gospel story, that doubt about His death was often in the Lord's mind. I think that as a rule, even though the future was not altogether clear to Him, He fully expected to die. When He said, "Except a grain of wheat fall into the earth and die, it abideth by itself alone ; but if it die, it beareth much fruit," He thought that it was by death that He would see His seed. When He said "I, if I be lifted up from the earth, will draw all men into Me," He did signify through what manner of death all the kindreds of the earth would remember and turn to God. But I think it to be true also, that at the last, when the abyss yawned before Him, and He felt suddenly all that it would mean for the Messiah to die, He faltered when before He had firmly trod, not in will, for that was ever one with the Father's will, but in the clearness of His grasp of what that will would demand. If so, it was very human, and it brings Him very near to us all. Of this at any rate we may be sure that, when He said, "Thy will be done," He said it in the noblest way, not pitifully or hopelessly, or even stoically, but knowing that the Father's will was a will for universal good, and loving that will because of all that it would do for us, His friends, for whom He laid down His life.

THE HOLY EUCHARIST

Maundy Thursday

"I have received of the Lord that which also I delivered unto you, that the Lord Jesus, the same night in which He was betrayed, took bread : and when He had given thanks, He brake it, and said : Take, eat : this is My Body, which is broken for you : this do in remembrance of me. After the same manner also He took the cup, when He had supped, saying : This cup is the New Testament in My Blood : this do ye, as oft as ye drink it, in remembrance of Me."—1 Cor. xi. 23-25.

HERE is our earliest account of the institution of the Holy Eucharist. When these words were written, not one of our Gospels was yet in existence ; but the holy feast of the Lord was being everywhere celebrated in the Christian Church. At Corinth, unhappily, it was not only celebrated, but profaned. So it is that St. Paul must write about it ; and, as the foundation for his teaching, tells his converts once more what it was that the Lord did and what the Lord said. Very solemn the Lord's action had been, very wonderful and mysterious His words. From the elder Apostles St. Paul has received the story, and as a treasure for all time he passes it on. Let the Corinthians consider it again. If they do, they will no longer profane the feast of the Lord.

I

Now it is this Holy Eucharist which we are to make the centre of our thoughts to-day. It is a characteristic of our Christian Faith that it forms one great whole ; every truth which it contains throws light upon every other truth, and is in its turn illuminated by it. And how great is our need

of a better understanding of the Eucharist, both for our
own sakes and for the sake of our witness to the world!
It is true that we must not wait for full understanding
before we draw near to the Lord in His Holy Sacrament.
He said, "Do this," not "Think this"; and if we do as He
commanded in remembrance of Him, we are sure of His
blessing, though it may be but little which we as yet understand. But none the less we should, through the Spirit,
as St. Paul says, seek to "know the things that are freely
given to us of God"; and to many of us, I think, our communions would be new things, sources of a new joy and
power, if we understand better what we ought in them to
expect, and by faith to claim. It is but a very simple
beginning that I shall try to make to-day. I shall not
touch on points of present controversy; I shall not speak
even of the Real Presence or of the Eucharistic Sacrifice.
Rather, we shall try to go back to the night in which the
Lord was betrayed, and to enter into His mind, so much
wiser than our own. Why did He institute the Holy
Eucharist, and why did He institute it then?

II

It is the evening of Maundy Thursday; and the lights
are already lit in the upper room, where the Apostles have
prepared the last meal of the Lord. It is in the house
probably of Mary, the mother of John Mark, the house which
will soon be the first meeting-place of the Christian Church.
One by one the Lord and the Apostles climb the stairs;
they enter and take their places on the low divans round
the table where the meal is laid. Is it a Passover feast?
Not precisely, I think. We hear nothing of any Paschal
Lamb; and the Passover of the Jews will take place
to-morrow on the evening of the first Good Friday. But
it is a pro-Passover, if we may so say; our Lord anticipates
the Passover for His little company, since when the
true Passover comes He will no longer be with them. It
is the Passover, at any rate, which is in the Lord's mind.

He is the true Paschal Lamb ; He will die as the Paschal lambs died in Egypt long ago, to preserve His people from death, that they may inherit the divine kingdom.

But are the Apostles thinking of this ?   Very far from it.   They are looking forward to an approaching triumph. All through His ministry the Lord had proclaimed the kingdom of God, the good time coming ; and the Apostles expect it immediately.   Much have they abandoned for the Lord's sake.   They at any rate have not gone, one to his farm, and another to his merchandize.   They followed the Lord when He bade them follow Him ; and they have stayed with Him ever since, though others have fallen away.   But their reward, so they think, is coming now. The Lord will reign, and they will reign with Him.   Who will be the greatest ?   Who will sit in the highest place at the coronation banquet ?   Who will be prime minister in the coming kingdom ?   And the Lord—He, too, looks backwards and forwards.   Yes ; they have indeed given up all for Him, and He loves them for what they have endured.   "Ye are they which have continued with Me in My temptations."   Their reward will come ; their office will be high in His Church here, and in the world to come blessings more than they can yet understand.   "I appoint unto you a kingdom, as My Father hath appointed unto Me ; that ye may eat and drink at my table in My kingdom, and sit on thrones judging the twelve tribes of Israel." But how long it may be before the final kingdom dawns ! It is His own last night on earth.   Never again on earth will He sit with them at the board ; never again pass the loving cup from hand to hand.   He is going to His death ; for without His death there can be no kingdom for Him, and no kingdom for them.   How will it fare with His little company ?   What will become of their faith, and hope, and love ?   Satan has asked for them, as he asked for Job in the old poem, that he may sift them as wheat.   The Shepherd will be smitten, and the sheep of His flock scattered abroad.   And, though God will bring again the great Shepherd of the sheep on Easter morning, they will see Him but a few times after His Resurrection, and soon He will be hidden from their eyes. Will they not in time forget Him? When the Son of Man comes, will He find faith on the earth? They are together now, but will they hold together after He has gone? Will they continue to look for the coming of the kingdom, or despair of it when its coming is delayed?

Well! the Lord's wisdom finds a way, and He finds it in the holy feast of which we think to-day. That old Passover of the Jewish people—how much it had done for them! Long ago God delivered them out of Egypt, and the Passover had been their feast of remembrance. Year by year they had kept it in remembrance of Him and His work of redemption. How much it had helped them, scattered as they had been, to remain one nation! To-morrow, not in Jerusalem and the Holy Land only, but in the far-off ghettos of Alexandria and Corinth and Rome, they will keep it again as the sacred people of God; and through it they will cherish God's promises to them, and continue to look for their fulfilment. That is the way. The Lord's company also shall have their Passover. Yes! the Lord will die, and it is one of His Apostles who will betray Him. But till He comes again, His Body sacrificed, His Blood poured out, will be the food and drink of a new Paschal feast continually celebrated by His people. So they will never forget Him. So they will still hold together as one family; the Eucharist will bind them one to another, as well as bind them all to Him. So hope will never die. His death will be proclaimed till He comes again; and, when He comes, there will be a Church to welcome Him.

III

These are great thoughts. They are the thoughts of the Lord Himself, if I rightly understand Him; and we must try think His great thoughts after Him. How great was His wisdom! What a wonderful remedy He found for the perils of His little company! Who would have expected the

Church to last, if age followed age, and the Lord did not return ? And yet it has lasted. The little company which met in the Upper Room has become a great company which no man can number, and still the feast lives on. Still by it we remember the Lord ; still we hold together as His family ; still we cherish the great hope one day to be realized. What a place the Eucharist has held in the life of the Church ! Soon, indeed, was the Upper Room too narrow for it. Whit Sunday came, and three thousand were added to the Church. The Eucharist was for them all imme-diately. "They continued steadfastly in the Apostles' doctrine and fellowship, and in the breaking of bread and the prayers." Then the Church goes out into the world. Orientals of every kind, Greeks, and Romans are gathered into the Church. But they are all one in the common feast. If for a moment things go wrong at Antioch, if Jewish Christians will not eat with Gentiles, and St. Peter seems to justify their action, St. Paul will not tolerate it for a moment. To refuse to eat together means to refuse to communicate together, and that must never be. St. Paul won the victory, and it was a lasting victory. Listen to St. Ignatius of Antioch, as he writes some seventy years later : "Take care to observe one Eucharist ; for there is one flesh of our Lord Jesus Christ, and one cup unto union with His Blood ; there is one altar as there is one bishop . . . that whatsoever ye do, ye may do it after God." Week by week, or even day by day, the feast is celebrated. The deacons take the Holy Sacrament to the sick. The hermits carry it away with them into the wilderness. Ever the Holy Eucharist remains the support of faith, the pledge of love, the promise of the coming glory. Do we not need it in all these ways to-day ? We too need it that we may more continually remember the Lord. We too need it to draw us all together, Catholics in the Church of England who think in one way about our present difficulties to Catholics in the Church of England who think about them in another, Catholics in the Church of England to Catholics of other communions, and Catholics everywhere to those

who do not prize that name as we do, but who yet love the
Lord Jesus Christ in sincerity. We too need it in an age
absorbed in the things of this world that, like the Lord, we
may look beyond it to that eternal feast of which He spoke.
Shall we end with that thought to-day ?

> "Thou art coming ; at Thy Table
>   We are witnesses for this ;
> While remembering hearts Thou meetest,
>   In communion, clearest, sweetest,
> Earnest of our coming bliss :
>   Showing, not Thy death alone,
> And Thy love exceeding great,
>   But Thy coming, and Thy throne,
> All for which we long and wait."

The great lover of our Lord who wrote these words was
not what we should call a Catholic ; she did not think of
the Holy Eucharist, I feel sure, as we do ; but she understood one thing about it which we sometimes forget ; she
knew that it was the earnest of our coming bliss in the
heavenly country, the promise and anticipation of the
marriage-supper of the Lamb.

SERMON XII

THE EVENING OF GOOD FRIDAY

GOOD FRIDAY EVENING

"And all the multitudes that came together to this sight, when they beheld the things that were done, returned smiting their breasts."—LUKE xxiii. 48.

IT is over; our Lord is dead. The priests, the elders, the crowd that shouted "Crucify", have had their will. Never will Jesus of Nazareth trouble them again. But observe what happens. Over the crowd that has come out to see there descends a pall of horror and foreboding. They cannot bear to look at the Cross with its "tragic loading". O God, that it had not been done !

I

Well! with us all it is the evening of Good Friday. Shall we all look back, and try a little to understand ? Why did we do this thing ? I say "we" advisedly, for the Jews were our representatives ; in a true sense we all were there. What was it in Jesus that men could not endure ? They followed Him at first in their thousands. They welcomed His gospel the coming kingdom in which all their ills would pass away, and of the free forgiveness of the Father in heaven. Still more did they welcome His miracles of healing, which made their homes so different from what they had been. All at first was as bright as a marriage feast. But the trouble lay here. Jesus was so one with God, so stood for God, spoke for God, acted for God, that he made upon men all the claims for repentance, for trust, for obedience, for sacrifice, that God must ever make. The kingdom of God means the rule of God ; if God does not rule us, neither can He bless. That is where the pinch always comes. When God asks to rule us, we all with one consent ask to be excused. We have our positions that we want to maintain, our views that we want to spread, our ambitions that we want to satisfy. The God that we desire is a God who will be our servant to do what we want, not a God who calls us to be His servants to do what He wants. Popular religion prays "my will be done"; true religion prays "Thy will be done", and upholds us in doing it. If we are determined to do our own will, we find Jesus very much in the way, and we wish Him out of the way : we hate, as He said, both Him and His Father. That is why we crucified Him then, and crucify Him now. The Jews were no more monsters of iniquity than you or I ; they had their excuses. But they were wilful, selfish, and stupid ; and so to the Lord the Cross came. "Father, forgive them, for they know not what they do."

II

Now perhaps you may not agree with this. Shall we then mingle with the crowd on its homeward way, ask them why they did what they did, and whether they are satisfied with the result ? If I make them speak the language of to-day, it will not be to raise a smile, but to help you to see that they were men and women of like passions with ourselves, and that we might have done as they did.

We will begin with no less a person than Caiaphas, high priest of Israel in A.D. 29. Utterly weary he looks. Like the Lord, last night he never slept ; and his diplomacy has been a marvel. He has thought of everything, managed everything and everybody ; the Cross is his triumph. Pilate wanted to save the Lord ; Caiaphas to destroy Him. Pilate had the Roman empire at his back ; Caiaphas, as far as physical force was concerned, was helpless. But as we watch the game, we see that Caiaphas wins almost every trick. Yet how anxious and miserable he looks now !

"Why did you do it, Caiaphas ? Why did you so hate
Jesus of Nazareth ?" And Caiaphas answers, "Who says
I hated him ? What do you take me for ? I'm not one
of the godly ; I hardly gave him a thought till a fortnight
ago ; he interfered with me, not I with him. Why did
he interfere in the temple ? The temple was my business,
not his. But that was not why I had him crucified.
I did that, because it had to be done. Jesus of Nazareth
was a danger of the first magnitude. Look at what took
place last Sunday. He rode into Jerusalem with thousands
of the Galilean pilgrims shouting for the restoration of
David's kingdom. I don't say that he was preparing an
insurrection ; but that is neither here nor there. As High
Priest, I must consider the national welfare ; I may care
for my place, but I care for my nation a great deal more ;
and the choice lay between the nation's life and his. You
know what those cursed Galileans are ; it only takes a spark
to fire that tinder. Let an insurrection once begin, and
down will come the legions from Cæsarea and Antioch ; the
gutters will be running with blood ; and what little is left
of our national existence will be swept away. The only
thing to do in such circumstances is to strike at the head,
and strike at once ; and the whole nation ought to be
thankful that there was someone on the spot with brains
enough and pluck enough to see the thing through. You
may say that it was a dirty business ; of course it was.
I no more enjoy dealing with a dog like Judas Iscariot than
you would ; still less do I enjoy pretending that I am an
enthusiast for the Roman occupation. But in this world
you must take such measures as are open to you, and
employ such agents as happen to be at hand. For us in
our present weakness the only policy is to keep on good
terms with Rome. The existence of Jesus made that
impossible, and so he had to go. The charge of rebellion
was good enough for Pilate, just as the charge of blasphemy was good enough for the Pharisees, and the charge
of wanting to destroy the temple for the mob. My business
was to employ the arguments that worked."

And we say, "Yes, I see. And now your place and the national existence are secure ?" And Caiaphas replies, "Well! let us hope so ; but it's Rome that decides who is to be high priest. What is worse is that superscription that Pilate put over the Cross. If the mob get it into their heads that a new Judas Maccabæus has been done to death, there may be the devil to pay ; we may have an insurrection after all. I have done my duty anyway."

Thus far Caiaphas. And now we will question a very different person, Simon the Pharisee, of whom we read in the Gospel story. "Why was it, Simon, that you Pharisees supported Caiaphas ? I thought you hated these Sadducean high priests ; and Jesus at any rate shared your supernatural faith" ? And Simon says : "We acted, as we were bound to act, in the interests of religion. Take my own case. I had no prejudice against Jesus at first. I'm a liberal-minded man, and I asked him to dinner. But he showed no sense of the honour done to him. He had the impertinence to complain that he was not treated as a friend ; indeed he was quite impossible. He had never attended one of our Rabbinic schools ; he was not a bit of a scholar ; and yet he wanted to put everybody right, and thought that no one knew anything except himself. He wanted to upset everything and to alter everything. He not only criticized the decisions of far wiser men than himself, but the law of Moses itself was not good enough for him. He broke the Sabbath shamelessly ; the company he kept was a disgrace to anyone professing religion. I shouldn't like to tell you what happened in my own house, but even that was not the worst. The language he used about us Pharisees and our teaching was simply outrageous, while his claims for himself were nothing short of blasphemous. Now the law itself commands us to put to death a blasphemer. Of course, I don't defend the lies Caiaphas told, or the things he did ; for them Caiaphas is responsible, and not we. But I don't see how we could have interfered ; we could only pray that they might be over-ruled for good. If Israel does not stand for the law

of God, what does it stand for ?   We have trouble enough
with those wretched Galileans as it is, when we try to bring
them under the yoke of the law.   They say that they have
to work for their living, and that the law is a burden that
they cannot bear.   Instead of supporting us, as a religions
man would have done, Jesus of Nazareth took their side ;
and so he had to go."

And we say, "Yes, I see.   And now you will be able to
bring these newly converted Galileans to keep all the rules
the Rabbis lay down."   And Simon says, "Well ! let us
hope so.   But these people who know not the law, are
cursed.   We shall send them proper scribes, of course, but
I'm not sure that at first the crucifixion will not make the
task even more difficult.   It's a bad business, but we did
what we could."

Thus far the great people ; now for the small.   Here is
a working-man on the way back, and no one could look
more miserable.   "Tell me," we say, "why did you and
your pals cry "Crucify" this morning, and ask for Barabbas
instead of Jesus ?   I know you had seen but little of
Jesus, but you had heard Him in the Temple, and I thought
you ordinary people heard Him gladly."   And he says,
"We did an' all ; he gave it to those Pharisees proper.
But, you see, we had to do it.   Do you know what he
brought up those Galileans to do ?   They were going to
destroy the Temple.   Caiaphas told us so ; he said we
might take it from him.   Do you think we were going to
stand that ?   Why ! people come from all over the world
to see our Temple ; and quite apart from religion, though
I'm a religious man myself, if there's one thing we're proud
of, it is that.   We'd nothing against Jesus otherwise ; we
didn't even know that he'd been arrested.   We came out
because it was Passover Day, and we wanted to get
Barabbas out of gaol.   Barabbas is a man ; he's popular
down here ; we'd got a bit of a feast ready for him.   D'you
think we were going to be put off with anyone else ?
Not likely.   What we want is to get these Romans out of
the country, and Barabbas is the sort of man to do it."

And once more we say, "Yes ! I see. And now that you have got Barabbas out, you'll be able to get on with the job." And he says, "Well ! let's hope so. Barabbas didn't bring it off at the last insurrection, and that's a fact. If only Jesus of Nazareth would have led us ! But what's the good of talking ? His notion was that if a man strikes you on the one cheek, you should turn the other : what's the good of that, I ask you ?"

III

Now, do you think that the Jews were such monsters of iniquity ? Punishments were crueller in those days than in our own, but everybody was accustomed to them, and thought little of their cruelty. Apart from that, do you think that we should have acted very differently ? I am a teacher of religion myself, and I ask myself this. If anyone had publicly attacked me, and my religion, and all the teachers of it whom I most respect, with half the force, and half the wit, and half the success, with which the Lord attacked the Pharisees, how should I have felt about it ? If I had been a Pharisee, with the prejudices of a Pharisee, in the Jewish National Assembly, should I have voted with Caiaphas or with Joseph of Arimathæa ? I wonder. Shall we all put to ourselves similar questions ? And then, having tried to answer them, shall we all put to ourselves a further one ? When we find Jesus in our way now, how do we deal with Him ? Among His traditional sayings, this is one : "He that is near Me is near a fire." If we are near Him, He does not let us alone. He interferes with our politics, our trade, our pleasures—yes, and as the Pharisees found, with our religion too, for sometimes we have a religion that is worse than none. When He interferes, as He is sure to do, how do we take it ? Look at it in this way. If we are Christians, His life is within us ; for, not only was it given for us, but by the Spirit it is given to us, and it is that life that interferes. It stands in the way by which we wish to go, and it says, You can go by that way, if you insist, but you must crucify Me first. I shall no more resist than I did at Calvary ; you may do as you will, and I shall be in your way no longer.   There are two ways of killing me.   You may do it slowly by a long course of carelessness, refusal of My calls, and little sins of which you do not repent.   You may do it quickly by one great deliberate sin.   But remember that first Good Friday evening.   When the deed is done, will you be happy about it, or will you go down the hill of Calvary under the same pall of horror and foreboding which the Jews felt long ago ?

EASTER RECKONING

"Christ being raised from the dead dieth no more ;
death no more hath dominion over Him. For the death
that He died, He died unto sin once : but the life that He
liveth, He liveth unto God. Even so reckon ye also yourselves to be dead unto sin, but alive unto God in Christ
Jesus."—ROM. vi. 9-11.

So God speaks to us on Easter Day. Once the burden of
sin was laid upon our Lord ; once He was under the
dominion of death. But it is not so now. The burden of
sin has been rolled away, and the dominion of death
destroyed. Christ is risen, and we must rise with Him.
"Reckon ye also yourselves to be dead unto sin, but alive
unto God in Christ Jesus."

I

It was indeed a true inspiration which brought the three
Easter Antiphons together ; they form the noblest canticle
in our English Prayer Book. The first deals mainly with
the past, the second mainly with the present, and the
third mainly with the future. If we understand them all,
we require little more for Christian faith and Christian
living. Let us think of the second to-day ; what does it
mean ? St. Paul has been speaking of Holy Baptism. In
baptism the Roman Christians had been made one with
Christ, and in a true sense shared His experience of death,
burial, and resurrection. What had the Lord's death been
to Him ? It was, as has been well said, "a perfect response
to the Father's love, a perfect surrender to His will, a
perfect repudiation of sin in every form and at every cost
to Himself" ; rather than sacrifice His obedience, He

97

G

sacrificed His life ; and it was through His sacrifice that
He rose to that higher and fuller life that He is living now.
So it had been also with the Roman Christians.   In their
baptism they responded to the love of God revealed to
them, they surrendered themselves to His will, they died
to the old life of sin.   Their plunge beneath the water of
baptism was their burial, their rising out of it their resurrection to a new life to be lived for God ; they not only
promised this new life, but received the power to live it.

Now it is this great thought of union with Christ in His
experience which lies behind the text, and we should notice
one of the changes which the Revised Version has made.
It says "alive unto God in Christ Jesus", not "through
Christ Jesus".   No human language is adequate to describe
our union with Christ, but "in" is here better than
"through."   The word reminds us that we are related to
our Lord, not just as disciples to a Master, or as subjects
to a King, but as a branch is related to the tree of which
it forms a part, or as a member is related to the body to
which it belongs.   The sap of the tree passes to every
living branch ; the member lives by the life of the whole
body.   "I am the vine," the Lord says ; "ye are the
branches . . . apart from Me ye can do nothing."   But if
we are in Him, not apart from Him, in Him we can do all
that He calls us to do.   "I can do all things," says St.
Paul, "in Him that strengtheneth me."

II

But do we recognize the present position of the Lord,
or what we in Him can be ?   We recognize, I think, the
first but partially, and the second very little.   If this be
so, we miss much of the joy of Easter.   Let me show you
what I mean.

Consider first the life, and so the joy of the Lord Himself.
Our Easter hymns rightly lay stress upon the glory of the
Lord, but not always with much understanding of its
character :

"Now above the sky He's King,
Where the Angels ever sing."

Is that our conception of living unto God ? I do not think that it was His. Certainly we should rejoice that our Lord's suffering is over, and His glory won.

"He has outsoared the shadow of our night ;
Envy and calumny and hate and pain."

But these thoughts of rest after toil, peace after pain, belong rather to Easter Eve than to Easter Day, to the dead rather than to the living ; and our Lord is risen from the dead. To what did He look forward ? Was it not to that true, though not spectacular, glory of which the prophet spoke ? "He shall see His seed, He shall prolong His days, and the purpose of the Lord shall prosper in His hand. He shall see of the travail of His soul, and shall be satisfied : by his knowledge shall my righteous servant make many righteous : and he shall bear their iniquities." He thought of His Passion, not merely as a cup to be drained because the draining was His Father's will ; but as a baptism by which He would pass to a higher and fuller life, in which He would reproduce Himself, like a grain of wheat, in a vast family who would be like Him, and forward the Father's purpose as He could not do while He was still under the limitations of this world. Now those limitations have passed away, and all power is His in heaven and in earth. What is the meaning of the words which tell us that death has no more dominion over Him ? Is it not that His powers never grow old and fail, as ours do, but are to-day as fresh and living as on the first Easter morning ? What is the meaning of the words which tell us that the life that He liveth He liveth unto God ? Is it not that all these powers are ever being employed in the service of God and for the forwarding of His purpose ? The Lord, as we shall see, is our sacrifice still, but a living sacrifice. There is no joy in idleness ; and there is no other man so active as He.

Consider, secondly, our life and joy in Him. We too in Him may be dead to sin, and alive to God. Just as a father, when he rises in the world, raises all his family with him ; just as a general, when he wins a victory, wins it for his army and for his country ; so the Lord's rising is our rising, and His victory our victory. We must see to it that, when He has "won the war," we ourselves do not "lose the peace." It is true that our bodies do not yet feel the touch of His risen life ; we grow more and more conscious, as we grow older, that we must "wait for the redemption of our body." But, to use St. Paul's language again, though "the body is dead because of sin," the spirit "is life because of righteousness" ; in our spirits we live by the risen life of Christ, and we must believe it and act upon it. How we misunderstand St. Paul's word "reckon" ! We think that to reckon ourselves as dead to sin means to imagine ourselves dead to sin. But to imagine and to reckon are very different things. I may imagine that I have a balance at the Bank. But the clerk who deals with my account does not imagine, but reckons, and I find how very different the two things are. Imagination has to do with fancy ; reckoning has to do with facts. So it is with our death unto sin, though here it is imagination which is depressing, and facts which are uplifting. To reckon ourselves as dead indeed unto sin, but alive unto God is to consider the facts of our union with Christ, and the power which it gives to us, and to act accordingly. What we imagine is that in greater or less degree we are still under the power of sin, just ordinary people of whom not much can be expected, and for whom the highest Christian life is out of the question. But the facts are that, if we are in Christ, we are not under the dominion of sin ; we are extraordinary people, and the highest Christian life is fully within our reach. Easter says to us "Don't imagine ; reckon." Be like the man whom the Lord had cured of the palsy, and told to arise and take up his bed and walk. Since the Lord called him to do it, he reckoned that he could do it ; and, when he arose, he found that he could. "Awake, thou that sleepest, and arise from the dead."

III

And how, my brothers, shall we better lay hold of these truths which we so often forget ? There is no way so good as the right use of that holy sacrament to which we all are bidden to-day. "Christ our passover is sacrificed for us : therefore let us keep the feast." Does that mean that our Lord is no longer our sacrifice ? If He were our sacrifice no longer, we could not feast upon Him. His act of sacrificing is over ; but He Himself, our sacrifice, remains. Once a sacrifice, always a sacrifice, till the work is over for which the sacrifice is made. The bride gives herself to her husband on her wedding morning, but not just for a moment : she gives herself then that she may give herself always till death parts her from him. The soldier for a great war gives himself at the recruiting office to his country, but not just for a moment ; he gives himself once that he may give himself always till the war is over, and the victory won.

Let us look at this more carefully. The Lord's act of sacrificing is over ; He gave Himself so perfectly "once for all" that He never needs to give Himself again. This act of sacrificing we remember at every Eucharist, and give thanks for it, but we in no way repeat it. But the Lord, our sacrifice, remains. Wherever He is, in heaven above or in earth beneath, there is His sacrifice, for His sacrifice is Himself. "It is finished"—Yes ! but not as a song is finished, which being sung passes away to live only in memory :

> "The song from beginning to end
> I found again in the heart of a friend."

It is finished as a Cathedral is finished—finished that it may abide for our continual use and blessing. The life that He liveth He liveth now to God for us ; as St. John says, He is, not merely was, the expiation for our sins.

"My faith looks up to Thee,
Thou Lamb of Calvary,
Saviour Divine."

Up—that is the right word ; not looks back to Thee, but up to Thee. We repeat what our Lord told us to repeat, not His act of sacrificing, but our use of His sacrifice. Our Lord's work was done so perfectly, that it never needs to be done again : ours is done so imperfectly, that it needs to be done again and again. We plead His sacrifice for the living and the dead, because in the living new sins are ever needing it, and in the living and dead alike new heights of sanctity are ever to be won by it. We feed upon His sacrifice again and again, that His life may grow strong within us, that we my indeed be dead unto sin and alive unto God, and go forth to prove it. Jesus is risen :

"He is a presence to be felt and known,
In darkness and in light, from herb and stone,
Spreading itself where'er that Power may move
Which has withdrawn his being to its own ;
Which wields the world with never wearied love,
Sustains it from beneath, and kindles it above."

Those words, like others I have quoted from the same poem, were not spoken of the Risen Lord. But they are not true of him of whom Shelley wrote them, while they are true indeed of the Risen Lord. If He, the eternal Word or Wisdom through whom the world was made, is to be found in herb and stone, much more is He to be found in the bread and wine, through which He brings His abiding sacrifice near. "Wherefore do ye spend money for that which is not bread, and your labour for that which satisfieth not. Hearken diligently unto Me, and eat ye that which is good. Incline your ear, and come unto Me ; hear and your soul shall live. . . . Seek ye the Lord while He may be found, call ye upon Him while He is near : let the wicked forsake his way, and the unrighteous man his thoughts : and let him return unto the Lord, and He will have mercy upon him ; and to our God, for He will abundantly pardon."

—1

SERMON XIV

THE DOCTRINE OF THE TRINITY

TRINITY SUNDAY

"The grace of the Lord Jesus Christ, and the love of God, and the communion of the Holy Ghost, be with you all."—2 COR. xiii. 14.

So ends St. Paul's great Epistle, and so has ended our service to-day. We see the Holy Trinity, not as a problem, but in close connexion with our personal needs. The grace of our Lord Jesus Christ, and the love of God, and the communion of the Holy Ghost—if these three things are ours, we have all that we need to glorify God here. and to be happy with Him for ever.

I

To-day is Trinity Sunday—God's own Sunday, and you will expect me to speak to you of the mystery of the Trinity. But do not hope that I shall make all clear to you. Only what is fully understood can be fully explained, and no one can fathom the nature of God. Can we then know anything of Him ? Yes, we can know all that here we need to know. But we must look at the experience we have had of Him, and see what the facts tell us. The Father, the Son, and the Holy Ghost cannot be directly known ; God dwells "in light unapproachable." But the grace of the Lord Jesus Christ, the love of God, and the communion of the Holy Ghost, St. Paul and his converts knew by their own experience, and we may know them too.

Now there is something strange at first sight about our

text. St. Paul seems to put the Persons of the Trinity in the wrong order. As a rule we put the Father first. "The Father," the Lord says, "is greater than I." The Father is, so to say, "the fountain of Godhead" ; the Son and the Spirit receive their Godhead from Him. But St. Paul puts our Lord first ; "the grace of the Lord Jesus Christ and the love of God." And the reason is surely this. St. Paul is thinking of the order of our own experience ; and he had known the grace of the Lord first. Our Lord had met him on the road to Damascus, and revealed His grace to him ; it was ever to St. Paul the marvel of the Lord's grace that He had called a persecutor and blasphemer to be His Apostle. Then through the grace of the Lord he had come to know the love of God, and from the Father and the Lord he had received the Gift of the Holy Ghost. That, as we shall see, is the true order for ourselves also ; the grace of the Lord Jesus Christ comes first, the love of God second, and the communion of the Holy Ghost third.

II

How was the grace of our Lord first revealed to us ? St. Paul tells us in this very Epistle. "Ye know the grace of our Lord Jesus Christ, that, though He was rich, yet for your sakes He became poor, that ye through His poverty might become rich." He came, a carpenter from Nazareth, and began to preach ; and all "wondered at the words of grace which proceeded out of his mouth". He said that God was about to establish His own rule in the world, and that under that blessed rule all our evils would pass away. Indeed, He began Himself to establish that rule ; there were acts of grace as well as words of grace. The blind received their sight ; the lame walked ; the lepers were cleansed, and the deaf heard. Nor were the acts of grace for the body alone. The Lord claimed to forgive sins ; He went even to the outcast to restore them to their place among the people of God. But He had not come only to minister, wonderful as His ministry was : He had come, he said, to give His life a ransom for His people. He would endure for us the Passion and the Cross; and by the way of the Cross He would be lifted up to the throne of God, and draw us all unto Himself. Moreover, what the Lord promised He performed; and in the result of St. Peter's first Whit Sunday sermon we see that the drawing has begun.

Secondly, how was the love of God revealed? In this way. When the grace of the Lord was revealed, the love of God was seen shining through it. It was from the Father that the Lord had come, and all that He did He traced back to the Father Himself. His message, He said, was the message which the Father had given Him to deliver; His deeds were the deeds which the Father had given Him to do; when He bestowed forgiveness, He bestowed it in the Father's name; His Death, and Resurrection, and Ascension, and Gift of the Spirit were stages in the accomplishment of the Father's will. And so St. Paul explains in this Epistle. "All things," he says, "are of God who reconciled us to Himself through Christ . . . Him who knew no sin God made to be sin on our behalf." You see how He traces all back to the Father, how He shows that, when Christ died for us, the Father commended His own love to us by what the Lord did. So he speaks again of "the light of the knowledge of the glory of God in the face of Jesus Christ." The glory of God is no external glory; it is the shining out of His saving wisdom, love, and power; and as we look at the face of Jesus Christ, and have experience of His grace, we find the love of God for us shining out indeed. Jesus Christ is not identical with the Father; no one can read the Gospels and suppose that He is. But it is from the Father's glory that He has come. In some mysterious way He so dwells in the Father, and the Father in Him, that we cannot distinguish between the word and action of the One and the word and action of the Other.

Thirdly, there is the communion of the Holy Ghost. When the early Christians knew and trusted the grace of

the Lord Jesus Christ and the love of God, they came
forward for baptism ; and the Apostles prayed and laid
their hands upon them, that they might receive the Holy
Ghost. Thus in this Epistle St. Paul says that God has
anointed and sealed us, and given us the earnest of the
Spirit in our hearts. Thus too he contrasts his own
mission with that of Moses, in that, while Moses brought to
men a law which condemned them, He was bringing to
men the Spirit of God who brings righteousness and life.
In early days, as among the Russians and Greeks to-day,
baptism and confirmation were hardly ever separated ;
they were two parts of one Sacrament, like the Gift of the
Body and the Gift of the Blood of Christ in the Holy
Eucharist. We speak of the communion—or common
sharing—of the Holy Ghost because the Holy Ghost is
God's great Gift to the Church, and every Christian is
meant to have his share in it. Moreover, when the Spirit
came, He was found, as the Lord had promised, to fill and
more than fill the place of the Lord Himself. He brought
illumination to the mind, and love to the heart, and holiness
to the life, and powers for service to God and man unknown
before. He was a gift from the Father and the Son, but
a living gift, dealing with men in a living and personal
way. Just as the Lord had been so one with the Father,
that His action was the Father's action, and brought the
Father near ; so the Holy Spirit was so One with Both that,
when He dealt with men, the Father and the Son were
dealing with them through Him. The mystery might be
great, but there was no doubt of the fact.

III

We see then the meaning of the text, reminding us as it
does how God has revealed Himself to us in our human
experience of Him. The doctrine of the Trinity is not just
a puzzle which we take on trust because the Church teaches
it, or because we can prove it from the Bible. It is just
that when we draw near to God, or when—perhaps we had

better say—God draws near to us to lift us out of our unhappiness and sin into the joy and purity of Christian life, we find that somehow—I cannot tell you how—God is Three and God is One. There is only one God, of course ; and yet, as our experience shows us, the Father is God, and the Son God, and the Holy Ghost God. That the Father is God goes without saying. But Jesus Christ is God, for no one but God could do for us all that He has done ; and the Holy Ghost is God, for no one but God could do for us what He is found to do.

What the exact difference between the Three is we do not know ; we say Three Persons, not because that is a satisfactory word, but because we have no better one to express what we want to express. But that need not trouble us, when the facts are clear. Indeed, when we look into our own mysterious nature, we find that we too are Trinities. Each of us has mind, and desire, and will, and yet each of us is one, and not more than one. Suppose that we go for a long country walk. Why do we do it ? Because we are Trinities—Three in One, and One in Three. First, there is the mind that knows. We know that May is the loveliest month of all the year, and that the flowers and trees are never so fresh and beautiful as now. Secondly, there is desire. We say, "I have been too busy all the week, but I should like to go and have a look at the country to-day." Then there is the will. We say, "When I have had my dinner, I shall go for a walk and see it." You see how that Trinity that we find within us all work together to send us out into the fields. Our human nature is a very mysterious thing, but that is the truth about how it works. Thought and desire and will are different things, and yet they all work together, and not one can act alone. I do not say that the Holy Trinity is like that, for God is a greater mystery even than we. But it would be very foolish to say that a Trinity is not possible, when we are all Trinities ourselves.

The last thing is this, and it is very practical. If we want to know God in our own experience, we must follow the path that St. Paul followed. We must begin with the grace of our Lord Jesus Christ. We must learn what He was, what He is, what He has done and can do for us to-day. Then, knowing and believing, we must see, shining behind and through it all, the love of the Heavenly Father ; and then we must go on to claim our share in the Gift of the Holy Spirit. We read that once at Ephesus, St. Paul found some very curious believers. He asked them, "Did ye receive the Holy Ghost when ye believed ?" and they replied that they had not even heard whether the Holy Ghost was given. Their baptism had only been John's baptism, and when St. Paul had given them Christian baptism and confirmation, the Holy Spirit came. I think that there are many to-day not unlike those Ephesians. They are satisfied with half a baptism—baptism not completed by confirmation—and seem not to know whether the Spirit has been given. Do not let us be among their number. And, if we have been not only baptized but also confirmed, and yet know little of the Spirit's power, it must be because we have never cared for, and trusted, and sought to hear the voice of the Spirit, or when we heard it have refused to follow it. Trinity Sunday is not only Trinity Sunday ; it is the Octave of Whit-Sunday, the Feast of the Spirit, and that is why to-day's Gospel speaks of the Spirit. If we have never received Him, we must seek Him in the appointed way ; and, if we have lost His presence, we must pray for His return.

THE QUEEN OF SHEBA

THE EIGHTH SUNDAY AFTER TRINITY

"Happy are thy men, happy are these thy servants, which stand continually before thee, and that hear thy wisdom. Blessed be the Lord thy God, which delighted in thee, to set thee on the throne of Israel : because the Lord loved Israel for ever, therefore made he thee king, to do judgment and justice."—1 KINGS x. 8, 9.

THERE is a special interest attached to those chapters of the Old Testament to which our Lord Himself refers. His use of them, His comments upon them, reveal to us His mind. Our first lesson spoke to us of Solomon's wealth, and of Solomon's wisdom ; and our Lord refers to both. Solomon's magnificence seems to have left Him cold. "Consider the lilies of the field, how they grow ; they toil not, neither do they spin : yet I say unto you, that even Solomon in all his glory was not arrayed like one of these." And Solomon's wisdom—our Lord does not seem to have been greatly impressed by that either. Human wisdom is a poor thing at best ; what He regarded as high and noble was the desire for wisdom, the willingness to take pains and make sacrifices to obtain it ; it was the Queen of Sheba who won the Lord's approval. "The queen of the south shall rise up in the judgment with this generation, and shall condemn it : for she came from the ends of the earth to hear the wisdom of Solomon ; and behold, a greater than Solomon is here."

I

These comments of our Lord are remarkable comments ; the writer of our Old Testament chapter would, I think, have been greatly surprised at them. I do not think that he set much store by the lilies of the field. What he admired was vessels of silver and gold, horses and chariots, lion-thrones, "ivory and apes and peacocks." The magnificence of Solomon was to him a source of national pride. So too was Solomon's wisdom. "He was wiser than all men," our writer says, "than Ethan the Ezrahite, and Heman, and Chalcol, and Darda, the sons of Mahol—those well-known authorities ; and his fame was in all the nations round about. And he spake three thousand proverbs ; and his songs were a thousand and five." Never would our writer have made the queen the centre of the picture ; he only introduced her to enhance the glory of the king.

And we—do we agree with our Lord's estimate ? We may agree with Him about the flowers. We have a love for nature and its beauty which the Jews never had ; we think the scarlet of the Encaenia a poor thing compared with the spring flowers of Wytham Woods ; and it delights us to see that our Lord felt as we feel. But wisdom ? Are we not further here from the Lord's mind than the writer of this chapter ? He at any rate put wisdom before wealth ; for, though wisdom sometimes leads to wealth, wealth never leads to wisdom. Do we Anglo-Saxon peoples know, as the great Jews have always known, that wisdom "is more precious than rubies" ; or is it with us, not, as with them, wisdom first, and wealth a good second, but wealth first, and wisdom nowhere ? Have you ever observed how small, in the highest subjects for thought, is the Anglo-Saxon contribution to human wisdom ? In science and invention the world owes much to England and the United States ; but in the higher wisdom how poorly we compare with Greece and Italy, with Germany and Spain ! And why is this ? Because far from believing that "the things which are seen are temporal, but the things which are not seen are eternal," we regard the things which are not seen as visionary, and the things which are seen as all-important. How little we care for wisdom ! How small are the time, that we will give, and the sacrifices that

we will make, in order to attain it ! When the Queen of
Sheba rises at the judgment to condemn our Lord's generation, will she not also condemn our own ? Shall we
think this morning of this saying of our Lord ? It is for
us very much to the point.

II

Let us notice first our Lord's exact meaning. It is the
margin of the Revised Version, not the text, which best
gives the meaning of the Greek. Our Lord says, not that
"someone", but that "something" greater than Solomon
is present in Himself. What then is this ? It is, I think,
the manifested wisdom and power of God—God's wisdom
enlightening our ignorance and folly, God's redeeming
power raising us out of our weakness and pain. So it is
that other words of our Lord seem to explain His meaning
here. "Blessed are the eyes which see the things that ye
see, for I say unto you, that many prophets and kings
desired to see the things which ye see, and saw them not ;
and to hear the things which ye hear, and heard them not."
Jesus had come, preaching the Kingdom of God, telling
men of the good time drawing near, when under the rule
of Almighty power and love all the evils of the world
would pass away.

But Jesus was not only the preacher of the Kingdom ;
He brought the blessings which He promised. The
Kingdom was already present in Himself ; His miracles
of healing were the first drops of the coming torrent of
grace ; the little band of followers which He gathered
round Him was the nucleus of the society in which the
Kingdom would begin to be realized, the mustard-seed
that would grow into the all-sheltering tree. How far
greater than Solomon was the wisdom and power of God
present in the Lord ! Solomon might be wise, but his rule
was far from bringing with it the rule of God : his very
magnificence, as we see if we read between the lines
of the story, was based upon the exploitation of his people's

toil. That was no true greatness. Jesus had no vessels of silver or of gold ; His teaching chair was no throne of ivory, but the bare hillside ; He came not to be ministered unto but to minister, and to give His life a ransom for us all. And yet, when He called, His people did not answer ; when He offered them the Kingdom, they all with one consent began to make excuses.

How is it with you and with me ? Do we profit by the Lord's wisdom ? His word is very nigh to us in the Holy Gospels ; "what sages would have died to learn" is "taught by cottage dames" ; and never man spake as He spake. How perfect is the very form of His speech ! It is limpid as the brook, yet deep as the sea. How striking are His epigrams, and how easy to remember ! How delightful is His humour, when He speaks to His friends ! How sharp the wit He can unsheath against His enemies ! How exquisite are His parables ! There is nothing like them in the literature of the world.

Or consider, not just the form, but the substance of His teaching. Think of His revelation of the Father. Who ever revealed Him as our Lord did ? Think of His teaching about the Kingdom—that Kingdom which begins in the Church here to be perfected in the life to come. Have you paid the toll for entering in ? Think of the character which He declares to be necessary for its citizens —humility, meekness, willingness to suffer, purity of heart, longing for the manifestation of the divine righteousness. Is that the character which you desire, or do you think it enough to be an English gentleman ? Think of the social principles which He lays down, the value of each human soul, the obligation of mutual service. Do you understand these principles, and seek to apply them ? Think of the two great commandments, love to God first, love to man second. Think of the unworldliness which He asks of us, of the Cross that He offers to us, of the great principle of dying to live. What are the proverbs of Solomon to all this, but as "moonlight unto sunlight, and as water unto wine ?" Truly blessed are our ears, if we

listen to our Lord's wisdom ; for something greater than
Solomon is here. But what a tragedy it is, if we prefer
the trash of the modern newspaper or novel to the gospels,
and know less of them to-day than we knew when we were
boys and girls at school !

Or consider, not what our ears may hear, but what our
eyes may see—"the house" that He has built for us, "the
attendance of His ministers", the "meat of His table", the
offering that He continually makes to the eternal Father.*
How poor and tawdry was all that the Queen of Sheba
saw, compared with what we may see to-day ! Think of
the marvel of the Church all down the ages, "the house
that He has built" to be our earthly home. Do you see
the marvel of that undying life, or do you take the Church
for granted as if it had been always there ?

> Crowns and thrones may perish,
>   Kingdoms rise and wane,
> But the Church of Jesus
>   Constant will remain.

Is that an empty boast ?   There are arches in this Cathedral
which were in their places before the English were one
people ; and the Church will stand when the British
Empire is "one with Nineveh and Tyre".   Why is it that,
in spite of all our folly and our sin, the gates of hell never
prevail against the Church ?   Or consider the "attendance
of His ministers", the long unbroken line of the Christian
ministry, which links us through the Apostles with the Lord
Himself, and compared with which the oldest families of
England are parvenus of yesterday.   Why is it that in
every generation men are found to give themselves to the
preaching of His gospel and the service of His sanctuary ?
What other cause claims such labour, while it offers so
little earthly reward ? Or consider the Holy Eucharist,
"the meat of His table", the one offering of the Lord and
of His people still pleaded with unfailing power.   Why do

---

*Cf. 1 Kings x. 5, R.V. margin.

H

we never tire of it? Why, though it divide us in our thought, does it unite us in our practice? Why do we still all alike do as the Lord did in remembrance of Him? Or once more consider the infinite privilege of Christian prayer—that prayer in which the least of us may lay all our "hard questions" before the Eternal Wisdom, and "commune with Him of all that is in our hearts." Why do we not cease to pray? What had Solomon to show compared with these wonders of the Lord? What was his temple compared with the temple of the Lord's body, the Church? What was his ivory throne compared with the altar of our King? Do you see these things? If so, blessed are your eyes. Or do you pass them by with some banal sneer at institutional religion? "Oh! yet consider it again." What pearls we despise when we turn and rend the Church which offers them! What a treasure we lose when we will not buy the field which contains it! Are not our Lord's words true? When the day comes when we must answer, not only for what we did, but for what we left undone—not only for the truth and grace which we had, but for the truth and grace which we might have had, how shall we bear the judgment of the Arabian Queen?

III

One thing more—the text. "Happy are thy men, happy are these thy servants, which stand continually before thee, and that hear thy wisdom. Blessed be the Lord thy God, which delighted in thee, to set thee on the throne of Israel; because the Lord loved Israel for ever, therefore made He thee king, to do justice and judgment." Beautiful words—like so many in the Old Testament, far too great for him of whom they first were spoken, but not too great for Him whom they fore-shadowed before He came; what do they say to us to-day? They say that the one satisfying proof of the love of God is that He gave for us the Son in whom "He delighted", and raised Him by the Cross to the throne of the world.

Do you believe in that love ?   I doubt if I should, if it were not for Jesus Christ.

> "Myself when young did eagerly frequent
> Doctor and Saint, and heard great argument
>   About it and about : but ever more
> Came out by the same Door where in I went.
>
> "There was the Door to which I found no key ;
> There was the Veil through which I might not see ;
>   Some little talk awhile of Me and Thee
> There was—and then no more of Thee and Me.
>
> "Earth could not answer ; nor the Seas that mourn
> In flowing purple, of their Lord forlorn ;
>   Nor rolling heaven, with all his Signs revealed
> And hidden by the sleeve of Night and Morn."

I think that if we were still of our Lord forlorn ; if there were no Divine Master before whom we might continually stand, and hear His wisdom ; no Church that He had built for us, no attendance of His ministers, no meat of His table, no abiding sacrifice, no communion with Him, we should falter, and never firmly tread ; and that our trust in the larger hope would be faint indeed.   And so He said, "I am the Way, and the Truth, and the Life ; no man cometh unto the Father but by Me."   Think of His "fame", so far greater than Solomon's, "concerning the name of the Lord."   Day by day, ponder His words. Live in the communion of His Church, the fellowship of His people.   Feed on the food that He has provided for you, and commune with Him of all that is in your heart. Then you will learn His love, and through it the love of the Father who sent Him.   You will make the dark queen's words your own, "Because God loved us for ever, therefore made He thee King to do justice and judgment."

THE ARMY OF GOD

THE ELEVENTH SUNDAY AFTER TRINITY, EVENING

"And his servant said unto him, Alas, my Master!
How shall we do ? And he answered, Fear not; for they
that be with us are more than they that be with them.
And Elisha prayed, and said, Lord, I pray thee, open his
eyes, that he may see. And the Lord opened the eyes of
the young man ; and he saw : and, behold, the mountain was
full of horses and chariots of fire round about Elisha."—
2 KINGS vi: 15-17.

HERE is the grand encouragement for the soldier. Hard
may be the fighting, while the conflict lasts ; times come
when all human help seems taken away, and our foes to
have us at their mercy. But always "they that be with
us are more than they that be with them". What we
need is that God should open our eyes to see it ; we shall
have no doubt of final victory then.

I

What an example we have in the great prophet Elisha !
Never perhaps has there been a time when God's cause
looked more hopeless than it looked in his day, and yet
seldom has there been a man who more splendidly fought
for it. What does fighting for God mean ? It means two
things. It means fighting for the Church of God against
the world that opposes it, and fighting for God within the
Church itself against the sin that disgraces it, and drags it
down to the level of the world that it is sent to win. Now
Elisha did both. On the one hand, as we heard to-night,
he was the champion of God's people Israel against their

enemies, worth more to Israel's king than all the soldiers
under his command. But then he was far more than this.
He was God's champion within Israel itself, the one man
in that poor decadent nation wholly on God's side, and
bringing the wisdom of God and the power of God to put
heart into it, and uplift its life. How like he was to the
Lord Himself ! Nothing was too great for him to do, and
nothing too small. Feeding the hungry and giving water
to the thirsty, healing the leper and reviving the dead,
comforting the poor woman who had lost her child and the
poor labourer who had lost his axe, moving about from
day to day, like the parish priests of England, among the
homes of his people, with deeds of mercy and with words
of cheer, the friend, the teacher, and the saviour of them
all ! If we would see what it is to be a man of God, we
have only to read the life of him of whom we have heard
to-night. To fight for God is to be, each of us, in his own
place, as Elisha was—to do, each of us, in his own place,
as Elisha did.

Now it is to this that God calls every one of us. Here
in the world to-day the Church of God is what Israel was
then. If we would fight for God, we must fight for His
Church. The Church is the witness that God has placed
in the world, the city set upon a hill for all to see. We
must keep it standing, and we must keep it strong. But
then that is only half our duty. We must fight against
evil within the Church itself. The Church of God must be a
holy Church. Its people ought to stand out against the
dark background of the world as a people doing the will
of God, and so enjoying an unexampled blessedness. And
the trouble is that the evil of the world is always getting
into the Church, and dragging it down to the world's level.
Thus we have a second work to do, at least as important
as the first. We have to maintain, as God's prophets of
old did maintain, a ceaseless war against the evil within as
well as against the evil without. If you and I are the soldiers of God, we shall have to deal, not only with the world,
but with those also who share with us the Christian cause,

but have not yet learned to exhibit the Christian character. That is what makes our task seem so hard for us. That is why sometimes God's best soldiers feel almost overwhelmed, and cry out, like Elisha's servant, "Alas! how shall we do?" Now I want, God helping me, to-night to do for you what Elisha did for his servant; I want to show you that "they that be with us are more than they that be with them." I cannot call up visions before you of horses and chariots of fire; perhaps it would not help you if I could. What I want to show you is the vast forces that are fighting on the side of God and goodness. I want you to see that it is not the servants of God who are outnumbered, but the enemies of God, and that if you cast in your lot fully and finally with God and His servants, you will be upon the winning side. May God open our eyes to see! That is all we need—to see things as they really are, and not as we in our discouragement think them to be.

II

So then to-night we will review the army of God, that we may see how great it is, and never be discouraged again. It is not only a great army; it is a very varied army. It has soldiers that we can see, and soldiers that we cannot see. But they are all part of the same army, and fighting for the same cause.

Now the first division of the army of God is a division that we all can see; it is nothing less than the world in which we live. This great and beautiful world was made by the great God, who is our Father. All the forces which it contains are His forces; all the laws which it obeys are His laws. God made it, and pronounced it very good. And therefore we may boldly say that the whole world is, and must be, on the side of those who are fighting for God. You know how great an advantage it is to any army to be fighting on its own ground. It is not merely that we know the ground; it is that we feel at home in our own country; and that every inhabitant, non-combatant though

he may be, wishes us well, and would help us to drive back
the enemy, if he could. Now that is our position. The
soldiers of God are fighting for God in God's own world.
If you are among God's soldiers, then the world itself, all
its forces and all its laws, are upon your side. Do you
think that this is a fancy of my own? Then listen to St.
Paul. "We know," he says, "that to them that love God
all things work together for good." Is not that a great
thing to remember? All things work together for good
to us, if we love God. And again he says, "All things are
yours; whether Paul, or Apollos, or Cephas, or the world,
or life, or death, or things present, or things to come; all
are yours; and ye are Christ's; and Christ is God's."
Yes—if we are really and fully Christ's, in heart and in
will, then all things are really and fully ours. It is not
only the servants of God, Paul, and Apollos, and Cephas;
it is the world too, life and death, things present and things
to come; all are upon our side. They are serving God
themselves, and in one way or in another they are all making
it easier for us to serve Him. It was said of the battle of
Megiddo that the stars in their course fought against
Sisera. The stars in their courses fight against the enemies
of God still; they fight by the side of His friends. You
see how the review is beginning; how the great army of God
is beginning to file past. "They that be with us are more
than they that be with them." I have heard of a man who
some years since was converted to God. He said that the
whole world was changed to him. Somehow, the sky was
bluer, and the fields were greener. So it may be with us
all. Perhaps there are some of you who have brought
here to-night the heavy burden of unforgiven sin. You
cannot feel at home in the world while that is so. Get rid
of it by true repentance, and you will find that the world
is changed to you. The stars above your head, the trees
waving in the park, the towers of the Cathedral rising up
into the sky, the very paving-stones under your feet—they
will all be different. The whole world will be to you, as
it was not before, a beautiful and friendly world; all things

will be yours, because you will be God's. What an army on the right side ! "They that be with us are more than they that be with them."

So then, the first great division has passed before us. Now comes the second ; and that is the army of the men and women now living and working who are upon the side of God. And that is a great army too—not indeed as great as it ought to be, but very great none the less. Never be discouraged because the servants of God seem to you to be few ; there are far more than you think. Do you remember how the prophet Elijah was discouraged just in that way ? "I have been very jealous for the Lord, the God of hosts ; for the children of Israel have forsaken Thy covenant, thrown down Thine altars, and slain Thy prophets with the sword ; and I, even I only, am left ; and they seek my life to take it away." Poor, discouraged prophet ! "But," as St. Paul says, "what saith the answer of God unto him ? I have left for myself seven thousand men, who have not bowed the knee to Baal." You see, Elijah added up the servants of God, and he brought out the grand total of one. But Elijah had done his sum wrong. God counted them too, and He brought out the total as seven thousand. Be sure that those who in their own way are faithful to God are far more than we know. "Be not afraid, but speak, and hold not thy peace"—so said our Lord to St. Paul in the wickedest city of his day ; "for I am with thee, and no man shall set on thee to harm thee ; for I have much people in this city." Never let us decry the place in which we live ; our Lord has much people in it. But they want encouraging, they want rallying ; and we are the people to do it. Take the right side boldly yourself, and others will take it with you. We drag one another down when we ought to lift one another up. Some of you have come to church to-night with friends who are sitting by your side. You perhaps have never spoken one word to help them to live for God ; they perhaps have never spoken one word to help you. And yet perhaps each of you is secretly longing for better things.

If either of you would be brave enough to speak first, you would find sympathy and help in the other. I remember reading of a man, who was leading with two friends of his a very careless life. He himself was very tired of it, but he found it difficult to say so. But he summoned up his courage at last. He said, "I think that if we go on in this careless way, we shall come to a very bad end." He did not much expect sympathy from the others, but he received it none the less. Instead of being forced to follow them, they followed him. In a little while all three were in the ranks of the clergy. Once more, those who are God's servants, or who wish to be, are far more than we know. What we need is to show our own colours, and then others will show theirs. But even when the servants of God are really few, there is no cause for discouragement, for each of them, if only he is whole-hearted, is a host in himself. Do you remember the words that Tennyson puts on the lips of the good knight, Sir Galahad ?

> "My strength is as the strength of ten,
> Because my heart is pure."

Yes, it is always so. Why is it, that, though God's servants always seem to be outnumbered, God's cause never fails ? It is because each man or woman, boy or girl, fully on the right side, is stronger than ten upon the wrong. God's servants love the cause for which they are living ; they love good for its own sake. But the devil's servants have no love for their cause ; not one in a million loves evil for its own sake. Any number of them would desert, if they saw their way to do so. Courage then, one and all. Even in this world of sin, "they that be with us, are more than they that be with them." Believe it, and show yourselves men upon the right side.

So then the second division has filed past. There is the visible world, and the visible men and women ; there remains the even greater and grander army that is not visible at all. And would that God would open our eyes to see it, as He opened the eyes of Elisha's servant of old !

What an army it is ! Let us lift up our hearts—lift them up unto the Lord—and see it as best we may. Here, in the Epistle to the Hebrews, is the roll-call. "Ye are come unto Mount Zion, and unto the city of the living God, the heavenly Jerusalem, and to innumerable hosts of angels, to the general assembly and Church of the firstborn who are enrolled in heaven, and to God, the Judge of all, and to the spirits of just men made perfect, and to Jesus, the mediator of a new covenant, and to the blood of sprinkling, that speaketh better things than that of Abel." And, my brothers, that great army on the side of God is only just out of sight. It is like the reserve divisions that a wise general keeps hidden out of gun-shot in the folds of the hills, ready to launch them at the enemy the moment that they are wanted. The regiments in the fighting line are bearing the brunt of the battle ; all the honour to them, if the reserve is never needed. But they know all the time that the reserve is there at their general's command, and that he is ready to use it. That is our position to-day. You and I are in the fighting line ; the immediate fortunes of the battle depend upon our steadiness and courage ; but the Lord, who directs us, does not depend upon us alone. The innumerable hosts of angels, the saints of God who have passed away, are only just out of sight. When the right moment comes, the Son of Man will send forth His angels ; He will come Himself with His saints, the "old Guard" of the kingdom of God, and the day will be won. How our Lord Himself believed in the great reserve when He was fighting here ! "Thinkest thou that I cannot beseech My Father, and He shall even now send Me more than twelve legions of angels ?" True, He never called for them ; H went into His battle to fight and to conquer alone. But He knew that the reserve was there ; He knew that, when He looked out from His Cross upon the savage crowd beneath Him, and saw not a friend among them all, even then they that were with Him were more than they that were with them ; and that, come what might, God would win.

III

You see then the greatness of the army of God. And now there is just this to say. Do we believe all this, and if we do, do we act upon it ? Soldiers of Jesus, do you believe that your cause will win ? You enlisted long ago—that is what your baptism meant ; are you fighting as those fight who have no doubt of victory, but who long to distinguish themselves before the battle is over ? Are you fighting as you should for the Church as a whole ? Are you fighting as you should against the evil within it ? My brothers, wherever you may be, at home or out in the world, at work or at play, in seeming danger or in seeming safety, you are absolutely safe if you are on God's side, and you are in mortal danger if you are not.

> The hosts of God encamp around
> The dwellings of the just ;
> Deliverance He affords to all
> Who in His succour trust.
>
> Fear Him, ye saints, and you will then
> Have nothing else to fear ;
> Make you His service your delight,
> Your wants shall be His care.

Yes, it is so. "They that be with us are more than they that be with them."

THE LETTER AND THE SPIRIT

THE TWELFTH SUNDAY AFTER TRINITY

"Who also made us sufficient as ministers of a new covenant ; not of the letter, but of the spirit : for the letter killeth, but the spirit giveth life."—2 COR. iii. 6.

THERE is a splendid enthusiasm burning in these words of St. Paul. In spite of all his sufferings, St. Paul was a happy man. And if we ask what made him so happy, we find the answer in our text. He had a splendid work to do, and God had made him able to do it. Those are the great sources of happiness. We cannot be happy if we have nothing to do ; we cannot be happy, even with work before us, if we are not able to do it successfully. But if we have a work to do that is worth doing, and can truly say, as St. Paul here says, that God has "made us able" to accomplish it, then we are sure to be happy without even thinking of it.

I

But it is not of the blessedness of work that I will ask you to think this morning. It is of that characteristic of the religion of our Lord which so filled St. Paul with enthusiasm. It is a religion not of the letter, but of the Spirit. What it gives us is not so much a law to reveal to us our duty, as a new power to enable us to accomplish it. Let us notice in passing that the contrast which St. Paul draws between the letter and the spirit is not the contrast which we ourselves are accustomed to draw between them. The letter of the law, we say, is one thing, and the spirit, the underlying principle, is another. When, e.g., our Lord says, "Whosoever smiteth thee on thy right cheek, turn to him the other also," we all understand that what He enjoins is not a particular movement of the head, but the patience and gentleness which that movement may be taken to express. What He meant we shall see, if we notice how He acted when He Himself received a blow in the palace of the high priest. He did not in any literal sense turn the other cheek, but He gave the gentle answer, "If I have spoken evil bear witness of the evil ; but if well, why smitest thou Me" ? Now this distinction between the letter of a law and the spirit of it, though capable of abuse, is sometimes of great importance. But it is not the distinction which St. Paul is drawing in our text. When he speaks of the letter, he does indeed mean a system of rules by which to regulate our lives. But when he speaks of the spirit, he does not mean the underlying principle of those rules ; he means the Holy Spirit of God, coming forth to us from our Lord Jesus Christ, and bestowing upon us a new ability to fulfil all the claims which God makes upon us.

Now that is an even greater contrast than the one of which we thought just now. "The letter killeth." The law of God condemns you since you cannot keep it. It takes the things which you are naturally inclined to do, and forbids them. It says, "Thou shalt not", and goes on repeatedly saying it. It takes no account of our weakness, no account of our temptations, no account of our circumstances. It just goes on forbidding, and threatening us with penalties if we disobey. What a contrast is presented by the action of the Spirit ! "The Spirit giveth life." He does not allow us to set aside the law of God—very far from that. He enters into us, and makes new men of us by giving us new light, and love, and power. And so what was impossible becomes possible, and what was difficult becomes comparatively easy ; and, as gradually we come to see more and more what God asks of us, we find ourselves continually able to accomplish it.

II

You see then what it was that so filled St. Paul with enthusiasm—what it was which made him feel that God had entrusted to him the most glorious mission in the world. His work was the ministration of the Spirit; it was to bring men through faith into union with our Lord Jesus Christ, so that from Him there might come forth to them this Holy Spirit who was to transform their lives. No doubt St. Paul carried to the Gentile world a higher moral teaching, but that was not the source of his enthusiasm. There was lofty moral teaching in the world before our Lord came. The Jews could give the world that; the Greek philosophers could give it; the great religions of the East could give it. But what they could not give was the power to carry out the moral teaching which they offered. They found the vast majority of men slaves to their passions, and to the evil surroundings of their lives, and they left them as they found them. Higher standards of living increased their unhappiness, by showing them the depth of their own degradation. But the power of Christianity lay in the fact that it could lift men out of their degradation. That was what St. Paul had learned out of his own experience. The Jewish Law only showed him what a slave he was; the Spirit made him free. And, wherever he went preaching the Gospel, and men repented and believed, and threw in their lot with the Church by receiving baptism, the same miracle followed. It did not matter what the previous life of his converts had been. They might have been, like himself, Pharisees of Jerusalem; they might have been dervishes practising the wild rites of Phrygia; they might have been Corinthian debauchees; but, if they received the Spirit, the Spirit made of them new men. That was the source of St. Paul's enthusiasm. The letter brought no deliverance; the Spirit brought a deliverance that was complete.

Now, my brothers, do you think that we grasp this distinction to-day? There are many, I think, who do not.

They have a most real belief in God, and they believe that
Jesus Christ was sent from God. But they regard Him
as if He were simply a great Teacher, in the same way that
Moses, and Muhammad, and Gautama, were great teachers ;
and, though no doubt they regard His teaching as higher
and truer than the teaching of anyone else, they still think
of His teaching and example as if that were all that He
had brought. Thus, when they hear in Church of what
goes beyond this, of Atonement through our Lord's death,
of union with Christ through the holy sacraments, of the
faith by which alone those sacraments can profit us, of
the necessity of prayer and corporate worship, what they
hear falls more or less upon deaf ears. They say that what
they want is something practical. It is the moral teaching
of our Lord that really matters, and as for these other
things, they may be all very well for people with a specially
religious bent, but they have little to do with practical
life. Now what I want you to see is that to say this is to
rob the Christian religion of its characteristic glory, and
to reduce it to the level of other religions. It is to make
it a religion of the latter, and no longer a religion of the
Spirit. More than this, so far from making Christianity
practical, it is to make it profoundly unpractical, so unpractical indeed that it is not worth preaching, and not worth
trying to practise. May I ask your careful attention to
this point ?

We regard then our Lord for the moment as the Teacher
of a noble code of morality. Let us consider how we stand
to it. We will put aside any of His sayings which may be
difficult to interpret, and confine ourselves to broad
principles. What then did our Lord say was the first and
great commandment ? "Thou shalt love the Lord thy
God with all thy heart, and with all thy soul, and with all
mind, and with all thy strength." We are, that is to say,
to be entirely devoted to God who made us. Our wills
are to be given to Him, our minds are to be fixed upon
Him, our hearts are to go out in love to Him, the whole
of our energy is to be thrown into His service. And the

second commandment, our Lord says, is like unto the
first : "Thou shalt love thy neighbour as thyself." The
interest, the happiness, the welfare of everyone with whom
we have to do is to be as dear to us as our own. And
observe that these two great laws are not merely to rule
our actions ; they are to rule our words and intentions
also.   Our Lord says that for every idle word we speak
we must give account at the day of judgment, and that to
speak words of contempt is to be in danger of hell fire.
He says that deliberately to foster the temptation to
impurity is one and the same thing with adultery itself.
Furthermore, it is not enough to do right; we must do
right with a pure motive. If we do right in order to be
seen of men, we have no reward to expect from our Father
in heaven. In a word, we are to be perfect, as our Father
in heaven is perfect. And, lest we might think that our
Lord does not mean all this to be taken seriously, He says
plainly that if our right hand or our right eye prevents us
from carrying out what He says, we must cut off the one,
or pluck out the other.

Now we are inquiring, you will remember, not whether
all this is admirable, but whether it is practical. Does our
Lord, while we regard Him simply as a moral teacher,
give us a religion which we are able to practise ? May I
speak simply for myself ? If this is what Christianity means,
I would rather be a Jew, rather be a Muhammadan, rather
by a Buddhist, than a Christian. It is not that I have
anything to object to what our Lord says. When He says
it, I can see that it is all true. Certainly I ought to do what
He says. My difficulty is entirely practical. I do not
feel myself either at all disposed, or indeed at all able, to
keep such a law as this. St. Paul may say that the law of
Moses condemned men, and slew them, but it was child's
play to this. The minute rules of the Pharisees might
have bored me exceedingly, but I think I could have made
a fairly successful Pharisee. But how am I going to be a
Christian ?   There is no doubt about it—"the letter
killeth". The law of Christ not only condemns us, but it

condemns us with a far deeper condemnation than the law of Moses did. And if Christ has brought us nothing more than this moral teaching, He is the most unpractical Teacher, and Christianity is the most unpractical religion which the world has ever seen. Consider a simple parallel. We heard in to-day's Gospel of a poor man cured by our Lord, who before his cure was deaf and had an impediment in his speech. Suppose that instead of curing him as the Gospel relates, our Lord had talked to him upon his fingers, and told him what a splendid thing it was to hear and speak, and that he must really set himself to speak plainly and to hear what his neighbours had got to say. Of what use would that have been ? It would have all been true, and our Lord would have said it all beautifully. But the people who brought the deaf and dumb man to our Lord would have felt that, if that were all that our Lord could do, they might just as well have stayed at home. And are we ourselves any better off, if all that our Lord does for us is to tell us what we ought to do, and ought to be, without giving us in any way the power to do and to be what He says ? Yes ! "the letter killeth". It condemns us and makes us long for something to raise us up into the true life, but it does not give us that true life itself. What we want is "the Spirit" ; it is the Spirit that giveth life; and how are we to obtain it ?

III

My brothers, there is for us, we believe, only one source of the Spirit of God, and that is our Lord Jesus Christ Himself. It is quite true that He is a Great Teacher, but He is far more than that. He is the Source from which there comes to us a divine Power, by which we can do what we should never do without it. What we have to do is in every way to draw near unto Him, and seek it from Him. How did our Lord really deal with that poor man, of whom the Gospel tell us ? He took him aside from the multitude—He wanted to get him quiet and alone.

I

He put His fingers into his ears, and took a little of the moisture from His own mouth, and touched his tongue with it. The poor man, of course, could not hear, but our Lord thus made him understand without words, that his deaf ears and stammering tongue were brought into the closest possible contact with the Lord Himself. Then, looking up to heaven, He sighed, and saith unto him, Ephphatha, that is, Be opened. The man might not hear the word, but he saw the Lord's eyes upraised to heaven ; he saw His breast heave as He sighed ; and then, when the Lord turned to him again, and he saw His lips moving, he knew that healing was coming, through his contact with our Lord. And straightway his ears were opened, and the string of his tongue was loosed, and he spake plain. And if we ourselves wish to receive from our Lord that power of the Spirit which will heal us, give us life, and enable us not only to know what is right to be done, but actually to do it, we too must come into contact with our Lord. That is why in the Church we have so much more than just moral teaching. We have teaching about all that our Lord has done for us, and sacraments whereby we can go away from the turmoil of the world to Jesus, that He may come into the closest contact with us, touch us, and heal us, and give us a power within ourselves whereby we may actually perform His will, instead of simply knowing what it is. Yes ! that is what we want. The letter—the rules—by themselves kill us. The Spirit of Jesus alone gives life.

Sermon XVIII

COVETOUSNESS

The Eighteenth Sunday after Trinity

"Take heed, and beware of covetousness, for a man's life consisteth not in the abundance of the things which he possesseth."—Luke xii. 15.

It was, as we heard this morning, an interesting incident, out of which these words of the Lord arose. His authority was widely recognized, and a man in the crowd thought that he could turn it to his own advantage. "Master, speak to my brother, that he divide the inheritance with me." Our Lord's answer was of lasting value. "Man," He said, "who made me a judge or a divider over you?" Here as elsewhere, if I understand our Lord aright, he upholds the authority of the State. Questions of property must always be decided by the State for this reason. It is only within the ordered State that rights of property exist ; there are none in the jungle ; and the State which itself creates and enforces these rights must decide what they are to be, and how far they are to go. Let us remember this to-day. If our Lord Himself had no mission from God to be a judge or a divider in such matters as these, the Church has none either. A Christian should be a good citizen, a supporter of the State in its proper work ; but he has a right to his opinions, and is neither necessarily a Socialist, nor necessarily an anti-Socialist. What he will say, and, before he says it to others, he will say it to himself, is what the Lord went on to say : "Take heed, and beware of covetousness : for a man's life consisteth not in the abundance of the things which he possesseth."

I

We think then to-day of covetousness—its meaning, its great evil, and its practical cure.

What is covetousness ? We are frequently in error on this point. Covetousness is a practical thing. It lies either in the effort to gain, or in the effort to keep, material goods unnecessary for the right support and development of our personal life ; and it is itself a sin quite apart from the other sins to which it may lead. Covetousness, as St. Paul says, is a root of every kind of evil. It leads to envy and hatred, when it cannot be gratified ; to fraud and cruelty, to self-indulgence and pride, when it can. But covetousness would still be a sin, if it led to no one of these other evils, a sin, as we shall see, against God, our neighbour, and ourselves. Consider the way in which our Lord spoke of the rich fool. The fool had not gained his wealth by fraud or violence ; it was entirely due to good harvests. His sin lay in the fact that, instead of using his superfluous wealth for the relief of others, he hoarded it, and would have used it to minister to his own laziness and self-indulgence. Now is this to some of you a novel and startling view of covetousness Do you doubt whether our Lord intended so to teach ? All down the Christian ages, if I mistake not, our Lord's followers have so understood Him. The Fathers, the teachers of the Middle Ages, the great moral teachers of the Church of England—all, as far as I know, speak here with one voice. They all deny our right either to seek, or to retain, material goods for which we have no proper use. Let us observe why. Between the higher goods of the mind and spirit, and material goods, there is this great difference. The supply of material goods is limited, while that of the higher goods is not. The goodness, which you or I by the grace of God may attain, the knowledge we may acquire, the talents we may develop for music or for art, so far from hindering the goodness or knowledge or artistry of other men, actually aid their growth. To "covet earnestly the best gifts" is a noble

covetousness. But material goods are, and must be,
limited in amount. If we lay up for ourselves treasures
upon the earth which we do not need, others must go
short ; and that is contrary not only to Christian charity
but to Christian justice. To say this is not to take a narrow
view of life, or to forget that God gives us richly all things
to enjoy ; to be a Christian is not to be a Puritan. All
that really makes for health of body, mind, and spirit, all
that truly enriches our personal life, all that is needed for
the fulfilment of our vocation, and the efficiency of our
work, all that makes for happy relations with those about
us, may be rightly desired ; and, though we often spend
far too much upon ourselves, that sin is not the sin of
covetousness. Nor, I think, do Christian moralists generally condemn a reasonable provision for the future. We
may be right to make such a provision for old age, as will
prevent our burdening others ; and right also to care for
the future of those dependent upon us, who will not be
able to support themselves. But, if we go beyond this,
we sin against God, our neighbour, and ourselves : against
God, because we are unfaithful stewards, and use what is
His in a way that His law forbids ; against our neighbour,
because, as we have seen, the superfluity of one means the
impoverishment of another ; and against ourselves, because,
as our Lord says, a man's life does not consist in the abundance of the things which he possesses ; and, if we are
covetous of material goods, we are certain to sacrifice
the higher ones.

II

Now we have here a vast subject ; there is but time to
deal briefly with one aspect of it—the aspect which appears
most distinctly in our Lord's words. The covetous man,
our Lord says, is a fool ; he understands neither himself,
nor the world he lives in ; and the more that, like the
Pharisees of old, he "derides" our Lord's teaching here,
the greater is his folly. God has given to each of us a great
and glorious nature, and material things will never satisfy

it. We are made for goodness, for truth, and for beauty ; made for eternal life with God, in whom all these things are found ; and, though our life upon its lower levels depends upon the right use of material things, it does not depend upon their being hoarded up. Thus to lay up for ourselves treasures upon the earth, instead of growing rich toward God by the use we make of them, is as great a folly as we can commit.

Consider the particular fool of whom our Lord speaks. A good farmer is a man worthy of all respect ; it is he, who under God provides the food upon which we all depend ; no one does more in the Son of Sirach's words to "maintain the fabric of the world". But our respect is based upon the greatness of his contribution to the common good ; and his willingness to promote it as long as he is able. Suppose then that, as in the parable, the one object of a farmer's work is, as soon as he may, to be delivered from the need of working ; suppose that the corn he grows is but to be stored in larger and larger barns, and to be used only for himself in a life of ease and self-indulgence ; how shall we respect him, and how will he respect himself ? Do you not see that in the moment that he says to his soul : "Soul, thou hast much goods laid up for many years ; take thine ease, eat, drink, and be merry," he condemns his soul to impoverishment and decay ? If he gives himself up to vulgar ease and riot, what kind of soul will be his in four years, if he lasts as long ? It is not only that "this night" his soul may be required of him ; then whose shall those things be that he has provided ? It is even more that the longer the time is which his soul is not required, the less of a soul it will be. That is the inevitable consequence of hoarding what we ought to spend. Where our treasure is, there will our hearts be also ; and as fast as the hoard grows, the soul that is tied to it dwindles and decays. Goodness, truth, beauty—these are the soul's food : only as we possess them are we rich toward God. To have a multitude of possessions, which we do not know how to use, is not to be rich, but to be vulgar, as everyone but the fool himself knows. We may grow a little weary of Punch's profiteers ; Punch harps upon that string too much. But Punch is right in representing covetousness as the vulgarest of all sins. A clever actor may present Sir Toby Belch or Sir John Falstaff as a gentleman, though a debased gentleman, but he cannot so represent Sir Giles Overreach. What is it to be vulgar ? To be vulgar is not to find oneself in a lowly position. St. Frideswide in a pig-sty was not vulgar, while Sir Gorgius Midas in a Rolls-Royce is. It is not to commit trifling solecisms in language and social custom ; such lapses are of no importance. To be vulgar is to be without true standards of value ; to think much of what is little, and little of what is much ; above all, it is to forget that, while the things that are seen are temporal, the things that are not seen are eternal.

And are the results of covetousness any better, if we are covetous not for ourselves, but for our children ? We only transfer the curse from ourselves to them. Will it be any less ruinous for them than for us to live without working ? Have we never observed that the man who has inherited "a competence" is generally incompetent, and that it is his competence which has made him so ? To train, to educate our children, to leave to them high standards of conduct and an untarnished name, these things are among our primary duties ; but why should we ever wish them to be "independent" ? Independent of what ? Independent of God, of the changes and chances of this mortal life, they can never be. Independent of their fellow-men—God forbid that they should be that either ! Always we must be members one of another, bound each to each by ties of mutual service. To be independent would be to be lonely—to live without fellowship and to die without love.

III

We see then the meaning and the evil of covetousness : what is its cure ? Are we never to make money ? Some people cannot help it ; their touch seems to turn everything into gold. The cure is, when our real needs are satisfied, to spend our money with a wise and noble generosity. I speak not only of those works of piety which not all can be expected yet to understand ; or even of those simpler forms of human service, which are open to us all. Are there not perhaps some here, of whom greater things may be expected ? There are in the New Testament two words of peculiar interest ; one is "Leitourgia", which we translate "service", and the other "Choregein", which we translate "supply". But what is their origin ? It is found in those public services, which the richer citizens of Athens performed for the State. One would provide a public banquet, another undertake an embassy, a third fit out a warship. So it was in later days. Wherever in the Roman world we find the ruins of an ancient city, there we find the remains of splendid public buildings, which the wealthier citizens supplied. How much we ourselves owe to the founders and benefactors of the Middle Ages I need not here say. Do you not think that "Liturgies" of this kind have more of dignity and beauty than can be found in a graduated income-tax ? Only, you see, if we are without the old national or local patriotism, if we do not understand that *noblesse oblige*, we must pay our toll in ways less honourable. There are rich men to-day, who do not fall short of the rich men of other days, as Bristol and other cities bear witness ; but might there not be many more ? We are fond of girding at Americans, and the almighty dollar. But the Americans not only know better than we how to make money ; they know better how to spend it, and are foremost in large works of charity throughout the world. It would be better here to imitate them than to gird at them. Then our elections might be something better than a struggle between the forces of envy backed by a good deal of wild justice, and the forces of covetousness backed by a good deal of sober commonsense. We might see again those golden days of which Macaulay speaks.

"Then none was for a party,
    Then all were for the State,
Then the great man helped the poor,
    And the poor man loved the great."

So may it be. At any rate, let us all "take heed and beware of covetousness: for a man's life consisteth not in the abundance of the things which he possesseth."

TEMPERANCE

The Twentieth Sunday after Trinity

"Be not drunken with wine, wherein is riot, but be filled with the Spirit; speaking one to another in psalms and hymns and spiritual songs, singing and making melody with your heart to the Lord."—Eph. v. 18, 19.

There is, I think, a real sympathy behind St. Paul's words. There are times when, in our modern phrase, we feel rotten, and want to be lifted out of ourselves; and wine for the moment will do what we want done. The man who has drunk more than he should is for the time exhilarated; he breaks into song without invitation, and continues without applause. Only, as St. Paul says, there is "riot" in this, which is undesirable, and there is the morning after. St. Paul suggests a better way. We should be filled with the Spirit of God. Curiously enough, there is a superficial likeness between a Christian filled with the Spirit and a man who has had too much to drink; it was noticed on the first Whit-Sunday, and St. Paul may remember this. The Christian filled with the Spirit is also exhilarated and lifted out of himself; he too is disposed to break into song, though into song of a more seemly character than is sometimes heard in the other case. There is however no riot, and no morning after.

I

Now in the Church of England we have been asked to-day to preach sermons on temperance; and I will do my best to comply with this request. Temperance is

extremely important for us all ; and there is wide misunderstanding of the teaching of the Bible and the Church
about it. When the Bible and the Church speak of temperance, the word is used in a wide sense ; temperance in the
use of drink is only one form of temperance. Temperance
in the use of food is at least as important ; indeed we need
temperance in the use of all our earthly blessings. Moreover, even if we narrow the meaning of the word to temperance in drink, the teaching of the Bible and the Church
is not what modern Puritans may have led us to suppose.
It is much more human and genial ; it is much more careful
in the statements which it makes. The Bible and the
Church are quite as much concerned for the welfare of men
as modern Puritans, but they conceive that welfare in a
broader way. I will try this morning to explain their
teaching, and then pass to that "still more excellent way"
of which St. Paul speaks in our text.

II

What then do the Bible and the Church teach with
regard to strong drink ? In Mediterranean lands wine is
the form of strong drink almost always in view, and the
Bible teaching is given in relation to that. This teaching
has two aspects.

In the first place, wine is regarded, not only as a good
gift of God, but as a rather outstanding gift. The one-
hundred-and-fourth Psalm affords us an example. "He
bringeth forth grass for the cattle : and green herb for
the service of man ; that he may bring food out of the
earth, and wine that maketh glad the heart of man : and
oil to make him a cheerful countenance, and bread to
strengthen man's heart." But it is not a question of a text
here, and a text there. Consider the place that the culture
of the vine holds in the whole Bible story. Much of the
land of Palestine was used for vineyards ; and that, not
primarily that grapes might be eaten, but that wine might
be drunk. Never once is it suggested that this use of the

soil was other than right and proper. So in the New Testament. Our Lord Himself drank wine, and ordained its use in the Holy Eucharist. St. Paul, in view of Timothy's health, advises Timothy to drink it. Abstinence from wine is indeed regarded as at times desirable ; but such abstinence is thought of, like abstinence from meat, as characteristic of the ascetic life, and belonging to the ordinary life only at special seasons. That a country should, in our modern phrase, go dry would have been to the Hebrews a thing inconceivable.

But then, of course, that is only one side of the Bible teaching. Though there is no rejection of wine, there are frequent warnings against drunkenness, as there are against gluttony. The misery, the poverty, the delirium that drunkenness brings ; the utter carelessness about higher things which follows upon it ; the degradation of our minds and the ruin of our souls which drunkenness inevitably causes ; these things are dwelt upon by the prophets and wise men of Israel with magnificent power. Drunkenness, Isaiah says, whets the thirst of the abhorred monster Death ; it makes her open her mouth without measure ; and the teeming multitudes of men, with their glory and pomp and joy, descend into it. Do not let us forget that, and take drunkenness too lightly. Wine rightly used makes glad the heart of man, though only for a little time. Wine abused makes man's heart unspeakably miserable, and not for a little time ; for no drunkard will inherit the kingdom of God.

Moreover, there is another point in the Bible teaching, which we may not have observed. The writers of the Bible do not, I think, regard wine as a thing that we should very freely use, even though we may never drink to excess. Its use should normally be occasional. It is doubtful whether alcohol is a food, and it is not a mental stimulant. It is a narcotic like tobacco, which may soothe our nerves, and so help us to sleep ; but it is not helpful when we have important work to do. The judge, so we read, should avoid it, when he is going to the bench ;

and the priest before the fulfilment of his sacred functions. It is in place at a feast, when we entertain our friends, just as better food is in place, and richer clothing than we generally wear. But feasting is not for every day. In a world like this, where there is so much suffering that we ought to relieve, and so many noble uses to which money can be put, it is selfish and vulgar to spend a great part of what we have upon things which perish in the using. Why did Dives in our Lord's parable lose his soul? Not because occasionally he was clothed in purple and fine linen, and fared sumptuously, but because he was so clothed and so fared every day. "What do you do with your old clothes?" a sensible man was asked; and his answer was "I wear them".

Now do understand the immense difference between one kind of expenditure and another. We may use money, as our Lord says, to lay up treasure in heaven, and to make friends for eternity; may bless by our use of it generations yet unborn. But even if we use it for ourselves, it makes a great difference how we use it. Suppose that you buy a horse or a picture. Perhaps you might spend your money better; but no waste takes place. The horse or the picture passes from the dealer to you, and so many guineas from you to the dealer. That is all. The horse or the picture on the one side, and the guineas on the other, are still part of the national wealth; it is only their position which has altered. But suppose that you spend your money upon a long succession of dinners or of wine-parties, which do neither you nor your friends any good. The food and the wine do not remain like the horse or the picture. They have gone, and no one has anything to show for them. To say that we should never spend more upon food or drink or clothing than is physically necessary is to go too far, farther than the Bible or the Church have ever gone. The best of us are imperfect as yet; and, if unhuman and unreasonable demands are made upon us, we may break away altogether. The way of the Bible and the Church is wiser and gentler. There are things that are definitely wrong, and they tell us so. But in many things no definite rule can be laid down, and the exact limits of personal expenditure are among them. Only, they tell us, as in the verses preceding our text, to look carefully how we walk ; not to be foolish, but to understand what the will of the Lord is. Food and drink are necessary to support us ; but if we take too much, we must support them. We should think oftener of the needs of others, and less about our own pleasures. We should see then that waste is not a form of generosity, but a form of meanness ; and with the facts before us we should judge rightly for ourselves what is the kind and human and rational thing to do. There is an old Jewish book, called the "Book of Tobit", which few of you may have read. It is a very odd book ; but as the framers of our Prayer Book knew, it contains gems of moral teaching here and there. Let me read you one. "Drink not wine unto drunkenness, and let not drunkenness go with thee on thy way. Give of thy bread to the hungry, and of thy garments to them that are naked ; of all thine abundance give alms." That is the best reason of all for temperance. Not that we refuse to make beasts of ourselves, or that we are afraid of the ills which intemperance brings ; but that we have not even now as much power to help others as we could wish ; and, if we spend much on food and drink and clothing, we shall have little indeed.

III

"Well !" you may say, "that's true enough. But if I cut down my pleasures too much, shall I not find life extremely dull ?" Yes! you will, if you go no further than that. There are people whose religion and morality seem chiefly to consist in the number of things which they don't do. They will go to heaven, we hope, but they are poor company here. But in our text the kind of religion which St. Paul recommends to us is a spiritual religion ; and a spiritual religion is one which, like drink, causes an almost irrepressible desire to sing. There are many ways in which the Gift of the Spirit produces this strange joy, but I will only mention one. Our happiness chiefly consists in liking what we are doing ; and we never do like it, unless it seems to us worth doing, and we have the power to accomplish it. Now the Spirit is given to us, when we believe in Jesus as the Son of God, and surrender our lives to Him ; and the man who is filled with the Spirit is always given by the Spirit a work to do, and the power to accomplish it. Exhilaration naturally follows. Again and again you will find that people who live the most strenuous lives and have a great deal of pain are remarkably cheerful ; while people who have nothing to do but to get a good time are plunged in the depths of gloom. That very often is why they drink. "Jesus Christ," it has been admirably said, "made wine, not a medicine, but a sacrament. But Omar Khayyám makes it, not a sacrament, but a medicine. He drinks, because life is not joyful ; he revels, because he is not glad." The Christian too may drink his glass of wine with his friends, when the day's work is done, but not for Omar's reason. He is happy already in the work that he is doing, and, please God, hopes to do. Let us eat and drink, for to-morrow we live.

Sermon XX

THE PEACE OF OUR LORD

The Twenty-First Sunday after Trinity

"Peace I leave with you ; my peace I give unto you ; not as the world giveth, give I unto you. Let not your heart be troubled, neither let it be fearful."—John xiv. 27.

Two things are here in close connection. On the one hand, there is a great gift. Jesus, our Lord and Master, as He leaves the world, bequeathes to us His peace. How His words bring out the greatness of the gift ! "Not as the world giveth, give I unto you." "Peace" was the common salutation in our Lord's day. When we should say "Good morning" the Hebrews said "Peace". But this with them was a wish, and nothing more. No one of us can give peace to the soul of another, near and dear though he may be. But with our Lord it was otherwise. When we only wish, He gave. That is the first thing in our text—a great gift. But the gift is followed by a command. "Let not your heart be troubled, neither let it be afraid." Gifts are intended to be used ; and if our Lord gives us His peace, He intends us to use it to quell those thoughts and expectations of evil, which render peace impossible. Here, as so often, we and God must work together. Though it is for Him to give, it is for us to cherish and use the gift. If we do not, very little will come of it.

I

Now it is of our Lord's peace that I would speak to you to-day. It is a peace of God passing all understanding, a peace that depends not upon outward circumstances, but upon a condition of our souls. All of us just now, I think, are feeling our need of it. Times, like these through which we are passing, not only try our manhood; they try our religion too; and we should not judge ourselves too harshly because it is so. If we grieve over the sufferings of others, Jesus Himself grieved over them also. If we are anxious about the future of our people, Jesus was anxious about the future of His own. It would be no sign of a Christian heart to pass unscathed through an ordeal like our own. Though the future is in our Father's hands, it is a future that may bring to many of us strain and suffering. In all our Lord has suffered with us; and I believe that He suffers with us still. But if our Lord gives us His peace, there should be in us a hidden depth of calm, though the surface be troubled. Our souls should be like the sea. There is a storm out in the Atlantic, and the waves run mountains high. But it is only on the surface after all. Down below, the fishes know nothing of it; all there is as calm as if no storm was raging. Now that is what we need both for ourselves, and for others, and that is what our Lord can give. Who ever lived a life so storm-tossed as our Lord Himself? Who was ever more a man of sorrows? Who ever bore such contradiction of sinners against Himself? And yet who ever enjoyed so deepseated a peace? It is His own peace that He bequeathed to us; He means us to be what He was. What then was the source of His peace, and how are we ourselves to lay hold of it? A great Christian teacher has said that in our Lord's peace there were three elements—peace of conscience, peace of character, and peace of trust. Shall we think of them all to-night, and see how we may attain them? All of them will make real demands upon us, but all are within our reach.

II

Now the first element in our Lord's peace was peace of conscience. He lived. He always lived, in unclouded communion with God. His soul was like the surface of a lake on some calm summer day, giving back the blue of the sky above it. Jesus was without sin, and so nothing ever dimmed to Him our Father's love. Father—Father— that was ever His word. We have it in His first recorded word : "I must be about My Father's business" ; we hear it in His last word upon the Cross. Amid the storms of life, the soul of Jesus was ever at rest, because He knew that the Father looked upon Him with approving love. He was the Father's beloved Son, in whom the Father was ever well-pleased. He was not alone, because the Father was with Him. My brothers, be sure that, if we would share our Lord's peace, we must begin by attaining peace with God. Jesus left us His own peace, because He had won by His Cross and Passion that peace for us ; and you and I must claim what He has won for us. You and I, it is true, know something that our Lord never knew ; we know the burden of past sin. But through His Cross we can, by repentance, get rid of it. We can repent of it, we can confess it—to our Father directly, and (if need be) to one of His ministers—and we can ask our Father to take it away. There will be no peace otherwise. With unrepented sin upon our consciences, not only are we afraid ; we have every reason to be afraid. Shall we not begin there ? It is useless to think of any other peace, unless peace of conscience is ours. Seek it, seek it by repentance, confession, and prayer for pardon. Get rid of the cloud which hides from you the face of God.

But then that was only one element of our Lord's peace. He had not only peace of conscience ; He had peace of character. That profound restlessness, which characterizes so many of us to-day, does not arise only from the fact that we are not at peace with God ; it arises also from the fact that we are not at peace with ourselves. We have no settled aim for our lives. We are full, not merely of unsatisfied desires, but of desires that are inconsistent one with another. Passion and inclination draw us one way, duty and conscience another. Indeed very often, as I said just now, our passions and inclinations draw us different ways. The love of pleasure comes into conflict with the love of

money, the desire for ease with the desire for the approba-
tion of those about us. How often we know the torment
of a divided and distracted mind! There can be no peace
in such a condition as that. The peace of our Lord did not
lie only in the fact that He lived ever in the sunshine of
the Father's face; it lay also in the fact that He ever
sought to do the Father's will. "My meat," He said—the
very thing that upholds Me, and keeps me alive—"is to
do the will of Him that sent Me, and to finish His work."
"I do always those things that please Him." It must be the
same with ourselves. There is only one thing which can
bring order into the wild turmoil of our desires, and that
is the submission of our wills to the will of God. We must
be ready, as our Lord was ready, not only to bear all that
we are called upon to bear, but to do all that we are called
upon to do. Our wills must be like the needle of a compass—always pointing one way. You take your compass;
you move it this way and that; and for the moment the
needle oscillates backwards and forwards. But it is only
for the moment. Place your compass in any position you
will; the needle will still point toward the north. That
is the picture of the man, who has what our Lord calls the
single eye, the man whose one desire is to do God's will.
Many longings come to him, as they come to others, and
for the moment they may disturb him. But it is only for
the moment. The will of God—his duty—the will of God
accepted and loved, masters the other desires, and brings
order and unity into his life; and so in the depths of his
soul he is at peace, like the Lord.

But there is a third peace, which the Lord possessed,
and which he bequeathed to us; and that is the peace
of trust. Just as the peace of conscience has to do with
the past, and the peace of character with the present, so
the peace of trust has to do with the future; and this
third peace follows inevitably from the other two. If we
have peace of conscience, and peace of character, the peace
of trust will follow almost as a matter of course. If we
are at peace with God, and doing His will, our future is

absolutely assured to us, and we can leave all with quiet confidence in our Father's hands. How beautifully the Psalmist describes the calm confidence of the servant of God ! "He will not be afraid of any evil tidings ; for his heart standeth fast, and believeth in the Lord." It is not that he knows that no evil tidings will come ; they will come again and again. It is that he knows that nothing can really hurt him if only his hand holds fast by the Hand of God. That was the Lord's way. All round Him, men were afraid—afraid for themselves, and afraid for Him. "Master, the Jews of late sought to stone Thee ; and goest Thou thither again ?" Jesus answered : "Are there not twelve hours in the day ? If any man walk in the day, he stumbleth not, because he seeth the light of this world." Beautiful words ! Yes ; there are the twelve hours of our life's day appointed for us ; we shall not stumble in them, if we walk in the light of God. There were times, even in the Lord's life, when for the moment He shrank back appalled at what seemed to be coming—do not let us blame ourselves if now and then we do the same. But, though He saw the Cross at the end of His journey, He saw also the Resurrection beyond it ; and He went His way entirely confident in the Father's care. That is the peace which comes to us, when our lives are given to do the will of God, and we can cast all our care upon Him. It is useless to tell us to trust God, if we are seeking our own wills and not His. The only man who can trust is the man who has a right to trust. But if our wills are His, and our purposes His, and our cause His, in the long run, we can no more fail than He can. And if that is so, what have we about which to be anxious ?

To do the will of Jesus—this is peace.

III

Peace of conscience then, peace of character, peace of trust. Is that all ! No, as we have seen, our Lord adds a command to His gift. "Let not your heart be troubled,

neither let it be afraid." Do you say: "Why, if our Lord
has left us His peace, is it necessary to say this?" Because,
in this, as in all other things, we must work with God.
It is not only necessary for our Lord to give; it is necessary
for us to take. Are there none of us, who have every right
to the peace of our Lord—every right because we have
repented of our sins, sought their forgiveness, and given
ourselves to do God's will—are there none of us, I say,
who have every right to our Lord's peace, but who are
continually anxious, continually troubled, as they certainly ought not to be? It is to these that the Lord here
speaks—to His followers, not to the world. He tells us,
indeed as our Master He commands us not to let our
hearts be troubled, or to let them be afraid. There are
wise words in the Book of Wisdom, which are much to
the purpose: "Fear is nothing else but a betraying of the
succours which reason offereth." Our Lord says to you
that, if you are at peace with God, and seeking to do His
will, you have every help, every encouragement, to confidence that can possibly be yours, in your knowledge of the
love of God and the certainty of His and your ultimate
victory. These succours you must claim, and you must
use, and not betray them to the enemies of your souls.
Prayer—continual prayer—that is the remedy. "In
nothing be anxious"—St. Paul commands us just as our
Lord does. "In nothing be anxious; but in everything
by prayer and supplication with thanksgiving let your
requests be made known unto God. And the peace of God,
which passeth all understanding, shall guard your hearts
and thoughts in Christ Jesus." That is the way. We are
to pray, thanking God for the past, and with all prayer
and supplication for the future. We are to cast all our
anxiety upon God, and not rise from our knees till we
have left it behind. Then we shall be at peace; within
the fortress of our souls, our hearts and thoughts will rest;
and the peace of God, the guard, the sentinel, whom God
will send, will pace up and down to challenge all that might
disturb us, and to tell us that all is well.

THE STIRRING OF THE WILL

The Last Sunday after Trinity

"Work out your own salvation with fear and trembling ;
for it is God which worketh in you both to will and to
work, for His good pleasure."—Phil. ii. 12, 13.

It is a call to action which St. Paul here gives to us. You
find, he says to us, a power within you, leading you first
to will, and then to accomplish, the will of God for you.
That power is God, nothing less than He. But does that
mean that you yourself have nothing to do, that you can
let your life drift, and God Himself will somehow bring
about your salvation for you ? Far from it. You must
work out your own salvation, and that with fear and
trembling. Just because it is God who is at work within
you, it is the more necessary that you should respond.
God's presence within you makes it certain that you will
succeed, if you mean to succeed. But you must really
mean it ; though God made us without our co-operation,
He will not save us without our co-operation. Our future
lies in our own hands. How deplorable it would be if, in
spite of God's presence with us, we were to miss our salvation !

I

Now there is a special reason for considering these words
to-day. This Sunday is the last Sunday of the Christian
Year. The world's year begins on the first of January,
but the Church's Year begins with the first Sunday in
Advent. We ought to be looking this week both backward
and forward—backward over the successes and failures of

the past, and forward with determination to do better.
How did our successes come ? By hearing God's call,
relying on His grace, setting ourselves to accomplish His
will. And how did our failures come ? Was it that God
never put into our minds good desires, or worked in us to
will what we were bound to do ? It certainly was not
that. We had good desires again and again. Was it that
when we resolved to carry out our good desires, and went
to work to do so, God failed us to support us in the effort
that we made ? It certainly was not that either. God
never let us down. His grace was always sufficient for us ;
we might have been more than conquerors. No, the failure
lay here that, though God worked in us both to will and
do, we refused to respond to Him ; that, though we knew
and desired what was right, we did not will what was right,
or did not will it with sufficient determination.

Now that is why in the Collect to-day we do not pray
for more grace ; it has not been the want of grace that
has caused the failure. But we say : "Stir up, we beseech
thee, O Lord, the wills of thy faithful people," for it is our
wills that have let us down. Stir them up ; wake them
from their slumber ; bring it home to us that we are men
and women who are capable of action and who are called
to action. Make us understand that if we want here and
hereafter to receive a plenteous reward, we must first
plenteously bring forth the good works that God requires
of us. We must not just dream about them, wish to do
them, plan them, and even make a beginning of them, but
bring them forth—actually get them done. It is true that
we can do nothing of ourselves ; that without God working
within us both to will and to do, we should never accomplish anything worth doing. As our Lord said, without
Him we can do nothing. But that is not the point of
which to think to-day. What we only too often forget is
the corresponding truth, that no kind of grace, and no
amount of grace, will conquer one single fault, or accomplish one single duty, unless we not only pray for grace,
but use it when it is given. Sending more grace to those

who do not use what they have is like sending more soldiers
to a bad general, or more money to a spendthrift ; it is
only more to waste. What is needed is first the stirring
of our wills, and then the active use of the grace of God
to accomplish the tasks committed to us.

II

Consider this first, as it affects the beginning of our
Christian life. In one sense, no doubt, it is never we who
begin. It is God Who "begins a good work" in us, and
seeks to "perfect it until the day of Jesus Christ". What
we do is always secondary, in response to what God has
done, and seeks to do for us. He has brought us into
His Church by Holy Baptism ; He has given us our
Christian homes, our Christian instruction, and the glorious
examples of our Lord and His saints. Nor has He been
satisfied just to call to us and help us from without ; as
St. Paul says, He has worked within us too. It was His
Spirit who lit up for us the truth that was handed on by
the words of others, who put into our minds good desires,
and called us to yield our lives to Him. God has a purpose,
that "good pleasure" of which St. Paul speaks, and all
along He has been working both without us and within us,
that His purpose may be fulfilled.

But will all this force us to be Christian men and women,
in spite of ourselves ? Certainly not. If it did, we should
be mere machines, and no longer men and women. God
draws us, as the prophet says, with the cords of a man,
even cords of love ; but, though He draws us, He does
not drag us. The age of decision comes : we must stir up
our wills and make it rightly. This Catholic faith, this
noble but arduous Christian life—shall we believe the one,
and live the other, or shall we just drift like thousands
around us, interested perhaps, more or less, in religion,
but never with the will stirred to come to any real decision
about it ? "How long halt ye between two opinions ?"
So Elijah said—"How long ?" It may be right to halt

for awhile, to learn more, to count the cost, as our Lord said, of the life to which God is calling us. But how long? —that is the point. We cannot balance things for ever, when a practical issue is before us. We have, in the phrase of Professor James of Harvard, "a living, forced, and momentous option". Ultimately it must be Yes or No; and, as long as we do not definitely say yes, we practically say no, even though we may not wish to do so. Suppose that one man says: "I shall not go abroad this year," and that another says: "I don't know whether to go abroad or not," what difference does it make which is said, if neither goes? So it is with believing the Catholic faith, and living the Christian life. Either we do, or we do not: not to decide for them is in practice the same as deciding against them. Indeed, indecision grows upon us. We decide nothing except not to decide. Yet every day in which we put off repentance makes repentance more difficult; and every day in which we still halt between faith and unbelief makes it harder to believe. Many of us have put off both too long already.

Consider it, secondly, as it affects our daily conflict with temptation. It is not enough to come out on the Christian side, not enough to be Catholic Christians. We have a battle to fight, and a work to do; and, though salvation is ours in germ and promise, we must work out our salvation with fear and trembling, or we shall miss it. Here too how much we need the stirring of our wills! Why is it that we have to confess the same sins again and again? Why is it that, though no doubt we should like to help the Church in the work that it is doing, somehow so little work gets done? It is not as a rule that we do not pray after our fashion, and use the means of grace; it is that in our prayers and sacraments our wills are not alive and active, and we have so little definite purpose in what we do. We pray and frequent the sacraments not to receive power for action and go out to use it, but supposing that to pray and frequent the sacraments are all the action that is asked of us. But that, as a great Christian writer has said, is to make them, not means of grace, but hindrances of nature ; we substitute them for the practical action we might otherwise take.   How differently our Lord taught us by word and by example !   "Work not," He said, "for the meat which perisheth, but for the meat which endureth unto eternal life."   "The kingdom of heaven suffereth violence, and the violent take it by force."   What man of will was He !   How full of fiery energy !   How clearly He saw the task that the Father had given to Him, and how ceaselessly He laboured to accomplish it ! "We must work the works of Him that sent Me while it is day : the night cometh, when no man can work."   And, when He used His power for other men, did He ask nothing of them ?   Did He not rather say : "Take up thy bed and walk" ?   If the man, to whom the Lord had given the power to rise, had lain upon his bed still, instead of arising, of what use to him would the power of the Lord have been ?   That is what we need—the stirring of our wills. It is of no use, as we look forward to the New Year, to hope for better things.   Hope is out of place in matters which rest with ourselves.   What we need is not hope, but determination, the clear vision of the task before us, and the steady effort, in reliance upon God, to get it done.   "Not everyone that saith unto Me Lord, Lord, shall enter into the Kingdom of heaven, but he that doeth the will of My Father which is in heaven."   There is no grace too great to ask from God, if only we mean to use it when it is given.   But if we desire a great grace, we must be ready to attempt a great task ; otherwise we shall receive the grace of God in vain.

III

And now there is just one thing more to say.   Remember that "there is only one way of beginning, and that is to begin."   Never mind about resolutions ; if the task is there, go at it at once.   A great psychologist has told us that, when we rise in the morning, there is not a second of time separating the effective resolution to get up, and being actually out of bed. The knock comes at our door, and there may be long delay before we obey the call that it brings. We may recognize that it is time to be up, that we ought to get up, that it is quite disgraceful that we still lie in bed ; we may even wish we were up. But none the less we still lie in bed. And then at last we find that we have sprung out of bed. There was no preliminary resolution ; we simply did what we ought to have done long before. And I say to you, my brothers, that if there is any decision that you ought to make now, any sin that you ought to overcome, any task that you ought to enter upon for the glory of God, you need not trouble about any resolution. What is wanted is just this—that you should do without any further delay what ought to be done. Pray for grace by all means, and be sure that what you ask you will receive. But don't wait until you feel stronger. Take up your bed and walk. And you will find that God Who worked in you to will, will also work in you to do, and that His grace will be sufficient for you.

Sermon XXII

FAITH AND FULFILMENT

The Annunciation

"Blessed is she that believed; for there shall be a
fulfilment of the things which have been spoken to her
from the Lord."—Luke i. 45.

We find here an abiding principle. God's promise is
one thing, and its fulfilment another : and the latter
depends upon our faith. The promise itself may be as
clear as that made to Mary, but the promise is not by itself
enough. Blessed only are those who believe ; for there
shall be a fulfilment of the things which have been spoken
to them from the Lord.

I

We see this first in the experience of Mary. The story
of the Annunciation is one of exquisite beauty, and surely
bears its substantial truth written upon its face. But
probably we should regard it as the story of a vision. Such
visions seem to be not uncommon when God calls His
servants to their appointed work : we find them both in
the Old Testament and in the New. The clothing of the
visions seems always to be drawn from the previous content
of the mind which receives it ; but the call which it brings
is a real call from God, and is shown to be so by the results
which follow its acceptance. This willing response is always
necessary, and always involves an act of faith. So it was
with Mary. The promise made to her was one difficult
to believe ; it was a promise of life, where the normal
conditions of life were absent. It was a promise also which,
though every Jewish maiden would welcome the call to

be the mother of the expected King, called for the endur-
ance of misunderstanding and pain. But Mary's faith was
equal to the demand made upon it. She said : "Behold
the hand-maid of the Lord : be it unto me according to
thy word" ; and so the Lord was born.

Now we find here the justification of the place which
belongs to Mary in the thought and love of the Church.
Devotion to Mary, as it is actually found in East and
West to-day, is no doubt largely heathen in origin. The
heathen who crowded into the Church, when Christianity
became the established religion of the Roman Empire,
had always had feminine objects of devotion, and Mary
took the place of the mother-goddesses and virgin-goddesses
of the heathen world. Thus devotion was paid to her
indistinguishable from that which had been paid to her
predecessors, and blessings asked from her as directly as
from God Himself. But devotion and love to Mary has
a Christian basis also ; for without her faith our Lord
would not have come.   That is why the Fathers speak of
her as the second Eve. As Eve, they say, by her disobedience brought death unto the world, so Mary by her
faith brought unto the world Christ, Who is our life :

> Her sacred name all generations bless,
> In that she ope'd the gates of Paradise.

How far our devotion should go, and what forms it should
take, are questions which we may not all answer in the
same way : I can see myself nothing but what is right and
beautiful in the *Ave Maria*, though I could not say the
same about the *Salve Regina*.

II

But it is not of this that I would speak to-day, but of
something more far-reaching. Did you ever notice that
in the Bible all the greatest acts of faith have the same
character ? We find in them the acceptance of a promise
of life where all the conditions of life seem to be absent.

Sometimes the life promised is for an individual ; sometimes it is for a nation or a Church. Sometimes it is a promise of supernatural resurrection. But the general character of the promise does not change ; and, when it is by faith accepted, the fulfilment takes place.

Consider first the stories of the birth and of the sacrifice of Isaac. We may regard them as strictly historical or we may not, but there is no doubt about their character. Not only is the first story one of supernatural birth, but the message of Gabriel looks back to it. The promise "no word of God shall be void of power" looks back to the promise to Sarah. Moreover, it is the faith of Abraham in God's promise of a son which St. Paul chooses as a typical example of faith. He "wavered not through unbelief, but waxed strong through faith giving glory to God, and being fully assured that what he had promised he was able also to perform." "He considered his own body now as good as dead"—"considered not" is a mistake of the A. V. ; he looked all the discouraging facts in the face. But he looked also at the promise of God ; like Mary he accepted it ; and so there was a fulfilment of the things spoken by the Lord. So it was also in the final test of his faith, the sacrifice of Isaac. Here, as the Epistle to the Hebrews explains, the faith was, not in a supernatural birth, but in a supernatural resurrection. The trial of Abraham's faith lay just in this, that on the life of the son whom he was called to sacrifice the fulfilment of God's promises depended ; and unless Isaac was to rise again, the promise and the sacrifice were incompatible one with the other.

Consider secondly the birth and sacrifice of Israel, the people and Church of God. What was the faith of Moses but faith in the new and supernatural birth of a nation, where all the conditions of life seemed absent ? That poor and enslaved people, Israel in Egypt, labouring under their task-masters, and hearkening not to their deliverer for anguish of spirit and cruel bondage, that people who, even when delivered, were continually murmuring under their hardships, and desiring to return to Egypt for the plenty they had there enjoyed, how could a great nation be created out of them ? Little wonder that in the old story Moses shrank from the call given to him, and could hardly be persuaded to respond. But he did respond, and there was a fulfilment of the things spoken by the Lord. Or consider the later history. What was the faith of all the greatest prophets but faith in a national resurrection when all true life seemed to have departed ? Think of Ezekiel's vision of the valley of dry bones, and of the national resurrection to follow. But Ezekiel does not stand alone. Isaiah, Jeremiah, the great prophet of the exile whom we call the second Isaiah, all exercise the same faith. They consider their people now as good as dead, the Northern Kingdom already destroyed, the Southern tottering to its fall, or already in exile. But they waver not through unbelief, but wax strong through faith, giving glory to God, and are fully assured that what God has promised He is able to perform. That wonderful picture of the Suffering Servant of the Lord which we find in the fifty-second and fifty-third chapters of Isaiah, is almost certainly in the mind of the prophet the picture of Israel or of its faithful remnant, despised and rejected of men, suffering and dying, and yet destined to rise and prolong its days that the pleasure of the Lord may prosper in its hand. It was in our Lord and His people that it has found its highest fulfilment, but it is not likely that the thought of the prophet reached as far as this.

Or, once more, consider the Lord Himself. Of the faith of Mary and of His supernatural birth we have thought already. But consider His own faith in His own resurrection. Whence comes that mysterious struggle in Gethsemane ? There may be depths here that we can in no wise fathom. But may we not believe that this last trial of the Lord's faith reproduced the last trial of Abraham's ? It was not the approaching suffering or death in themselves from which the Lord shrank back appalled, but from His own death, the death of the Messiah upon whom the fulfilment of all God's promises depended. He Himself felt "the offence of the Cross", as the Jewish people felt it after Him. If for the moment He thought that, when His self-surrender was perfected, the cup might pass away, was not perhaps the experience of Abraham and Isaac in his mind ? But, be that as it may, it was to a resurrection of some kind that His faith looked forward, though He may not have known what form it would take, and had himself to walk by faith, and not by sight. So He "offered up prayers and supplications with strong crying and tears unto Him that was able to save Him from death." In itself the Cross meant death, and not life ; there was nothing in it to suggest resurrection. But the promise was there, and He accepted it;   the fulfilment in due time followed.

III

Now there are two reasons for dwelling on these facts to-day, one relating to the faith of the Church and the other to our own Christian lives. We will take them one by one.

In the first place, you are probably aware how many to-day find it difficult to believe either in our Lord's birth of a virgin, or in His bodily resurrection and the empty tomb ; and I think we should sympathize with the difficulties they feel. Where there is little grasp of the teaching of the Bible and the Church as a whole, it is not surprising that the difficulties seem insuperable. But our Lord's answer to the Sadducees of His day is surely the abiding answer in both cases. "Is it not for this cause that ye err, that ye know not the Scriptures, nor the power of God ?" It is a gentle answer, as well as a profoundly wise one. If the Virgin Birth and the Empty Tomb appeared to me to be isolated and unintelligible marvels, I doubt if the evidence would force me to believe in their reality. I believe, partly because, though I do not know the Scriptures as I ought to know them, I know enough of them to see, not only that supernatural birth and resurrection are the characteristic forms which the manifestation of God's power has taken, and partly because they remain the characteristic forms in the Church to-day.

Now that brings us to the second point, that relating to our own Christian lives. How does St. John speak of Christians? They "were born" he says "not of blood, nor of the will of the flesh, nor of the will of man, but of God." The language is at first sight strange, but it surely shows two things. The first is that St. John believed the doctrine of the Virgin Birth though he does not speak about it, when he writes for Christians who have already been instructed in it ; and the second is that he regards the new birth by which we become Christians as corresponding to the supernatural birth of the Lord. Moreover, when we think of it more deeply, we see that our new birth by water and the spirit is also a resurrection. We must die unto sin first, and then we rise to newness of life. At first, the new life is in our souls alone ; it does not reach the body yet. But one day, if we are faithful, it will reach our bodies also. Only there must be faith in the divine promise. Blessed is every one who believes, for there will be a fulfilment of the things spoken from the Lord. What is it that the Christian convert should do, as he comes forward to baptism ? What is it that we all should do when first we understand what our baptism as children meant, or when after knowing once we have been unfaithful to our knowledge ? We should recognize that God is calling us to receive and to live by a supernatural life. We should look all the facts in the face. We should, to go back to the old words once more, consider ourselves now as good as dead ; but with the Scriptures and the power of God in view we should waver not through unbelief, but wax strong through faith, giving glory to God, and being fully assured that what He has promised He is able also to perform. If He calls us to new life, we are to say, "Be it unto me according to Thy word" and the new life will be ours.

Yes ! and what is true of us is true of our parochial life,

L

and of the life of the Church of England, and of the life of the Church Catholic throughout the world. The facts may be disconcerting ; and we should consider the facts, not refuse to consider them. But then, having done so, we should look away to the divine purpose and promises, and know that what God has promised He is able, if we respond to Him, fully to perform. That is what God asks of us ; nothing else "gives glory to God" as faith does. "The Son of God, Jesus Christ, who was preached among you by us was not yea and nay, but in Him is yea. For how many soever be the promises of God, in Him is the yea. Wherefore also through Him is the Amen unto the glory of God through us." The promise is God's, but the Amen which takes Him at His word is ours : and both are through Christ our Lord.

CHRIST, THE REVELATION OF GOD

ST. PHILIP'S DAY

> "Philip saith unto him, Lord, shew us the Father, and it sufficeth us. Jesus said unto him, Have I been so long time with you, and dost thou not know me, Philip? He that hath seen me hath seen the Father; how sayest thou, Shew us the Father? Believest thou not that I am in the Father, and the Father in me? The words that I say unto you I speak not from myself: but the Father abiding in me doeth his works."—JOHN xiv. 8-10.

IT is a familiar text that I have taken this morning, but it is one which makes a peculiar appeal to very many to-day. If God, they would say, is anywhere revealed to us, it is in the character, the words, and the works of Jesus Christ. We do not wish, as St. Philip may have wished, to see God revealed in a blaze of coloured fire. If we could so see Him, we should learn no more of His character than we had known before. It is God's mind and purpose that we need to know, and it is only in God's speech and action that we can know them. If then the words of Christ, as here we read, are not spoken from Himself, but are God's words; if in the works of Christ we see the Father abiding in Him, and doing His own works, we have only to understand these words and works to have the revelation we require: He that has seen the Lord has seen the Father. But now comes our difficulty. Do we know God apart from Christ, or do we not? If we know God before our Lord comes to us, why do we need His revelation? If we do not, how do we know that our Lord resembles Him? We cannot escape this difficulty, though we may ignore it; let me try to make it a little clearer.

I

Now there are, broadly speaking, two kinds of believers in our Lord's Divinity. There are those who are Theists first, and Christians afterwards ; and there are those who are Christians first, and Theists afterwards. We will consider these two classes in turn.

The watchword of the first is this : "Ye believe in God, believe also in me." We do not, they would say, derive our knowledge of God from the Lord alone. God was revealing Himself long before the Lord came. We learn of Him from nature, from history, and from conscience. We hear His voice in Old Testament prophecy, and follow His activity in His agelong dealing with Israel His people. We know that God is all-sovereign, and all-wise, and all-holy, and all-gracious. Thus, when we look at the words and works of the Lord and see all these attributes so wonderfully manifested in Him, we can but regard Him as God manifested in the flesh ; and say with St. Thomas "My Lord and my God." That on the whole is the line of argument of the older apologists. But in this case, though he that has seen the Lord has seen the Father, he has only seen more clearly and more movingly what he had seen before.

The watchword of the second class is this : "No man hath seen God at any time ; God only begotten, which is in the bosom of the Father, he hath declared him." We do not, these would say, see God anywhere but in Christ. The world of nature and of history, man as he has been and as he is, the chequered history of Israel as of other nations, reveal to us no God worthy of our worship ; we cannot tell what God may be. It is in Christ alone that we find one worthy of the name of God ; if we are Theists, it is to Christ that we owe it. That is the line not infrequently taken to-day, and it is one with which we should all have sympathy. Certainly there is much in nature, and more in history, which is darkness rather than light. But in this case, how can we argue from the character of Christ to the character of God ? *Ex hypothesi*, the view of God which Christ gives to us finds no confirmation elsewhere ; and, if this be so, ought we as rational beings to accept it ? At first sight this new apologetic is even less satisfying than the old. Though it lends itself to rhetorical expression, its logic is altogether to seek.

But does revelation take place by a logical process ? Is it not rather a matter of direct perception ? All great things must themselves be their own revealers, and declare both their existence and their character. We can learn but little of them from the words of others, however true these words may be. To one who has seen a sparrow we can describe a goldfinch ; when the goldfinch appears, it will cause no surprise. But not even Swinburne or Conrad can describe the sea : the sea itself must reveal the sea, both *that* it is, and *what* it is. The words of Swinburne and Conrad may no doubt be illuminating at a later stage ; they may lead us to a new appreciation of the sea ; but revelation must come from the sea itself. So it is with God. God may reveal Himself in many ways, but He Himself must deal directly with us : it is not enough, as Job declares, to hear of Him with the hearing of the ear.

II

There is a beautiful psalm, the nineteenth, which may guide our thoughts at this point. If it is composite, as our scholars tell us, the whole is far more than the sum of its parts. It begins with the witness of the world to God ; it turns from this to the witness of the law ; it ends with a cry of deliverance from sin.

First then, there is the witness of the world to God. "The heavens declare the glory of God : and the firmament sheweth his handywork." But how do they declare and show all this ? Do they reveal God by their very existence, or do they reveal Him by their order and their beauty ? The Hebrew poet does not draw this distinction. Indeed, there is no such thing as bare existence : whatever exists must exist as this or that ; it is orderly and beautiful, or the reverse. Now the world is a noble world, and witnesses to God in being so. The sun comes forth as a bridegroom from his chamber, and rejoices as a giant to run his course. And this course is orderly and invariable. "His going forth is from the end of the heaven," and he "turns unto the end of it again." And, wherever he goes, he blesses. "There is nothing hid from the heat thereof." Now this witness is a direct witness. It does not wait for theistic arguments to be based upon it, or for Kant to criticize them ; few things are more difficult than to put such arguments into a satisfying form. But the heavens do not argue with us ; they declare and show ; "their sound is gone out through all the earth, and their words to the end of the world" ; and, if we have eyes to see, and ears to hear, we receive their witness. Somehow, as St. Paul expresses it, "the invisible things of God are clearly seen, being perceived through the things that are made, even his everlasting power and divinity." Just as plainly as the heavens are seen by the bodily eye, so plainly are God's power and divinity seen by the eye of the soul, if, as our Lord expresses it, that eye is single. It is to the soul as a whole that the witness is borne, and not to the intellect alone. Indeed it is not, strictly speaking, the heavens which declare God's glory so much as God who Himself declares it ; we see, if we have eyes to see, both *that* God is, and something of *what* God is. If we fail to see, no argument will make it plain.

Secondly, there is the witness of the law to God. "The law of the Lord is perfect, restoring the soul : the testimony of the Lord is sure, making wise the simple. The precepts of the Lord are right, rejoicing the heart : the commandment of the Lord is pure, enlightening the eyes. . . . More to be desired are they than gold, yea, than much fine gold : sweeter also than honey and the honeycomb. Moreover by them is thy servant warned : in keeping of them there is great reward." There speaks the Pharisee at his best. The law of God is a revelation of God to His people Israel, which goes beyond that given to the world ; the law, even more than the world of nature, declares the glory of God. But how does it declare it ? Is it that we can frame out of moral experience an argument for God's existence and character ? Is the Psalmist anticipating Kant, or Butler, or Newman, or Sorley ? Their arguments we may follow with admiring interest, but we generally forget them. The revelation however does not come through argument, nor is it made to the mind alone. It comes in the immediate response of the conscience to the law, in the conviction that the statutes of the Lord are right. It comes in the power of the law to illuminate the mind, and rejoice the heart, and restore the soul. It comes, not in any external reward for obedience, but in the happiness which accompanies and follows it. In the keeping of the commandments there is great reward. In the authority with which the moral law speaks to us ; in its illuminating and restoring power ; in the joy, so far beyond all that we looked for, which follows obedience, God Himself draws near to us, and reveals both *that* He is, and *what* He is. He says not only "Ye therefore shall be perfect," but adds "as your heavenly Father is perfect."

The world then, and the law ; but now the shadow falls, for the Psalmist recognizes the fact of sin. "Who can discern his errors ? Clear thou me from hidden faults. Keep back thy servant also from presumptuous sins ; let them not have dominion over me : then shall I be perfect, and I shall be clean from great transgression." There lies the shadow : in the presumptuous sins only too possible for us, in the slavery into which we fall, in the wrong within of which we become all the more conscious, when we cease to sin with a high hand. God will only be fully revealed when He takes the shadow away. Indeed it has been present all the time. If the Psalmist forgets it in his praise of the sun, it is because he keeps his gaze fixed upon the sky, and does not bring it down to earth. We cannot separate the world from man to whom it all leads up ; and, if man himself fails to declare the glory of God,

the din and scandal of his wretchedness drown the witness
of earth and sea and sky. Indeed, it is only in the con-
sciousness of man that the world is known : its order, its
beauty, its utility, are order, beauty, and utility for him ;
and, if all is wrong with man himself, all is wrong also with
the world as he can know it. So with the law. If the
Psalmist forgets the shadow, it is because he thinks only
of the power of the law when it is fulfilled, and not of its
power when it is broken. In itself the law may be holy,
and the commandment holy and righteous and good ; but,
if we cannot observe it, it leads but to the bitter cry, "O
wretched man that I am ! Who shall deliver me out of
the body of this death ?" So it was that to the people of
God the greatest revelation of God was not that which
came through the world, or that which had come through
the law, but that which had come through God's redeeming
activity in their own history ; in their redemption from
Egypt and from Babylon, in that love of God which,
though He punished, always devised means that His
banished might not continue outcasts from Him. It was
in His redeeming activity that God had most clearly
revealed both His existence and His character. And,
when the Jews looked forward to a fuller revelation in the
great days to come, it was by a new redemption that they
looked for it. It was long before they came to hope for
any other world than this ; and they thought that there
was no more law left in heaven. But they did expect that
God, their Rock and their Redeemer in the past, would
redeem them again ; that they would see once more His
mighty Hand and stretched out Arm in works of grace and
power ; and that so, and not otherwise, God would give the
final revelation of Himself.

III

We see then that if the modern apologist denies that
God is known apart from Christ, he is far astray. The
Lord came not to destroy, but to fulfil. But we shall not,

as the older apologists may sometimes seem to do, regard God as already adequately known, and base our belief in our Lord upon the identity of His attributes with the known attributes of God. That would be to deprive our Lord of His true honour. Rather, God so perfectly reveals Himself in Christ to those who have eyes to see, so declares to us in Him *that* He is and *what* He is, that the older forms of His revelation, real as they are, are almost forgotten in the new. "That which hath been made glorious hath not been made glorious in this respect, by reason of the glory that surpasseth." We cannot see the stars while the sun is shining, though the stars are shining still. In Christ, too, God does not argue with us, but tells us ; and the light of the knowledge of the glory of God in the face of Jesus Christ, if we have eyes to see it, makes lesser light superfluous. Let us follow the Psalm again, and see how this is so.

Can we say that the witness of the world to God is all embodied in our Lord ? We often speak to-day as if our new recognition of the vastness of the world in space and time brought with it a new revelation of God. But is this so ? When man first gazed into the starry sky, and said to Him whom it revealed "What is man that thou art mindful of him ?" the world had done all to reveal God's greatness that it would ever do. God's greatness was inconceivable then, and it cannot be more than inconceivable now. If a million miles is more than our minds can grasp, we are no more impressed by a trillion than we are by a million. But in any case mere size has no value ; a nuisance is none the better for being a great nuisance, nor is a complicated machinery any better than a simple one, unless it does its work better. If man is "the paragon of nature", as Hamlet says ; if it is man to whom it all leads up ; what can nature have to teach us of God which is not taught by the perfect man ? It is God's character and purpose that we need to know ; and only the moral activity which belongs to man can reveal that. The Church sings the nineteenth Psalm on Christmas morning, greeting the Lord as the bridegroom coming forth from the womb of Mary, and rejoicing as a giant to run His course ; "from the great deep to the great deep He goes". And what a course it is that He runs ! He is *semper agens, semper quietus,*" ceaselessly at work through the twelve hours of the day, and yet ever at rest under the Father's smile. What an order and a beauty in the days of labour and the nights of prayer ! "Day unto day uttereth speech, and night unto night showeth knowledge." And yet, with all the order, what freedom and spontaneity ! What adaptation to changing circumstances, and to the variety of human characters and needs ! What a ceaseless devotion to the Father's work, and what ceaseless variety in the ways of forwarding it ! Is there any revelation of God which the world can offer us by its order and beauty that is comparable to this ? How little of God can a mechanism reveal, and how much the ever-changing response of the perfect man to the ever-changing needs of others !

But it was not in the Lord's character alone that the Apostles found God revealed, nor was it that which caused men to say "What manner of man is this ?" It was the Lord's authority, His wisdom, and His mighty works. Consider His authority. If the law brought with it a revelation of God, what shall we say of the word and teaching of Christ ? If the conscience responds to the one, how much more it responds to the other ! It is, as Tyrrell says, when the Christ that is outside us calls aloud to the stifled and buried Christ that is within us, *"Veni foras"*— Come forth, that our conscience is resonant to the call, and answers, and comes forth from the sepulchre to a new and supernatural life. Our Lord speaks as one who expects to be obeyed ; He not only claims authority—anyone can do that—but makes us feel that it is there. We may love His voice, welcome it, and try to follow it. We may be profoundly disturbed by it ; and, if we are not ready to follow it, depart in sorrow like the man who had great possessions. We may even be enraged by it. But we cannot despise it, or laugh at it, or be as if it had not been heard. In all this, even more than in the law, if we have ears to hear, God reveals Himself, shows us both *that* He is, and *what* He is. And if we obey, how much fuller becomes the revelation! The restoring of the soul, the making wise of the simple, the rejoicing of the heart, the enlightening of the eyes, the "great reward" of obedience— if the law bestowed these things, how much more does the Christ bestow them! If the one in this way was a revelation of God, how much more is the other!

Once more, consider the Lord's redeeming power. That new outburst of redeeming activity, by which the Jews had expected their God to crown all earlier revelation, was found alike in the life of the Lord, in His Resurrection, in His gift of the Spirit and in all that has flowed from it. How often we have been told in the last fifty years that the miracles of the Lord are to us to-day difficulties in the way of faith rather than supports to it! Could anything be further from the mind of Christ than that? Certainly He refused by meaningless wonders to force men to believe. But His mighty works were no meaningless wonders, but works of redeeming power; and He appeals to them in the Synoptic Gospels, just as in the Fourth Gospel, because they are this, because they are the first drops of that torrent of blessing which the Kingdom of God will bring. There is no contrast to be drawn between a work of mercy and an evidential miracle; it is power used in the service of love which constitutes its evidential character. In a world like ours, the world as we have made it, God cannot be fully God to us until He redeems and saves; it is precisely in restoring, in changing from the worse to the better, that He best declares *that* He is, and *what* He is. It was in healing the sick, in feeding the hungry, in stilling the storm, that God was revealed as God in the Lord's earthly life; it was in the power by which He raised the Lord from the dead, in the sending of the Holy Ghost to break the dominion of our presumptuous sins, and to cleanse us from our ingrained evil, that God was best revealed in

Christ's heavenly life, and is still revealed to-day. So the Lord teaches in our text : "He that hath seen me hath seen the Father. The Father abiding in me doeth his works. Believe me, that I am in the Father and the Father in me : or else believe me for the very works sake." Is the Lord appealing just to the marvel that His works present ? Not so. He is appealing to the fact that they are the Father's works, the works of the God who was expected to redeem, and to reveal Himself in redeeming, and who now in the Lord is actually redeeming. So with the Resurrection, the gift of the Spirit, and with all that has flowed from them. All are alike the revelation of God in redeeming activity—God not arguing with us, but telling us. Just in so far as the world is a world of order and beauty, God is revealed in the order and in the beauty. Just in so far as it is a world of hideous disorder, as by our fault it largely is, God is revealed in changing and trans- forming it with a mighty hand and a stretched-out arm. But the second way of revelation is far the fuller and more satisfying.

IV

Are then the two schools of believers and their watch- words so far apart ? May we not unite the truths for which they stand in a satisfying whole ? From the first school we shall take their conviction of the reality of God's revelation before our Lord came, and from the second their belief in its practical supersession by the light of the knowledge of the glory of God in the face of Jesus Christ. So with their watchwords. They are fully consistent the one with the other, if we rightly translate and rightly understand them. Our Lord did not say "Ye believe in God, believe also in me"—that would separate too much the Revealed from the Revealer : He said "Believe in God, and in me believe"—in the Father in whose house are the many mansions, and in the Son who goes to prepare a place for us. And when St. John says "No man hath seen God at any time ; God only-begotten, which is in the

bosom of the Father he hath declared him," he means that
God has never been seen by the eyes of the body, but that
what comes nearest to it is the revelation given in the
Lord; for that revelation is not by argument, made to
the mind alone, but one to be perceived by the whole
being of those who have the pure heart which can see God.
The Lord, like the heavens, does not demonstrate, but
declares the glory of God; and if, when we study Him, no
revelation comes, argument will be for us in vain. But,
as we have seen, great things must declare themselves;
and it is because the Lord is God only-begotten, that
He reveals the Father as He does. We do not know what
the eternal relation of the Son to the Father may be; "No
one," He said, "knoweth who the Son is but the Father";
the relation may not be one which human words can express, or human thought conceive. His Sonship is His
own secret; and it is only as it shines out in His word and
action that we are able to enter into its meaning. Perfect
unity with the Father, entire dependence upon the Father,
perfect representation of the Father to us—that is what
we find in Him; and yet so true a personal life that His
words and actions, though always the Father's, are nevertheless always His own. It is His very nature to be the
messenger and agent of the Father; and in all that He
says and does He and the Father are one.

There are words in St. John's Gospel which are the more
illuminating for the paradox which they present. "As
the Father hath life in himself, even so gave he to the Son
also to have life in himself." You see the paradox. How
can a life and activity wholly derived from another be
none the less His own? If the Lord's message is the
message given him by the Father, if He does nothing but
what He sees the Father doing, how is He more than the
Father's instrument? But, as we read the Gospels, we
cannot so think of Him. Though all is the Father's, all
is none the less His own. The Word of God "comes to"
the prophets; they say "Thus saith the Lord". But the
Word of God never comes to the Lord, for it is never absent

from Him ; He says "Verily *I* say unto you.　Heaven and
earth shall pass away ; but *my* words shall not pass away."
So with His redeeming activity.　It is all the Father's,
and yet it is all His own ; no one ever refused to be grateful
to the Lord on the ground that He was the instrument of
another.　"*I* will ; be thou made clean."　"Thou deaf and
dumb spirit, *I* command thee, come out of him and enter
no more into him."　"Young man, *I* say unto thee, arise."
"Peace, be still."　Nor is there any change in that larger
life that He is living now.　Still there is the same unity,
the same dependence, and the same representation.　The
life that He lives He lives unto God ; it is God who is in
Christ reconciling the world unto Himself.　And yet the
Lord is no mere instrument.　The Spirit which He pours
out upon us is His own Spirit ; the grace and peace which
are ours come to us from God the Father and the Lord
Jesus Christ ; and as He lives because of the Father, so we
live because of *Him.*　That is the mystery which we strive
to express when we say that the Lord is "God *of* God,
Light *of* Light, Very God *of* Very God."　He is like us in
this, that He has nothing but what the Father gives to
Him.　But *what* the Father gives to Him, and has given
from eternity, is Deity—the Deity which we adore.

Sermon XXIV

JESUS ONLY

The Transfiguration

"Jesus only with themselves."—Mark ix. 8.

It is a strange and disappointing experience which these words describe. Such great things the Apostles had seen, and yet for so short a time. Jesus, that mysterious Master, who was so slow to declare Himself, had at last been seen in His glory. Elijah, the great forerunner of the Kingdom of God, had at last seemed to have come— Elijah, and Moses with Him. Yes! and there had been something further still. The Voice, which had spoken on Sinai, had been heard again. "This is My Beloved Son; hear ye Him." Everything had seemed ready for that forward movement for which they were looking. Ah! now at last the King will come into His own. Here, on the mountain, will be the headquarters of His conquering host. Here will be the tabernacles for Moses and Elijah and the Lord Himself. Here once more will be the cloud of the Divine Presence, as of old in the wilderness, and the Voice of the Lord God ready to speak from it to the wondering people. And then in a moment they "look round", and the vision has fled. How we seem to hear in St. Mark's narrative the very words of St. Peter, as he spoke in after years of the bitterness of his disappointment, "No one any more, save Jesus only with themselves." Just the well-loved way-worn form of their Master, and the old patched garments, and no glory for the bodily eye shining out from either. Just Jesus only with themselves, the old selves that had failed before, and might fail again. Then the slow descent from the mountain, and their lips sealed for the time as to what they had seen, and at the foot the old dull world with its human miseries. Yes! they must be patient—intellectually patient and morally patient—for the triumph will not be yet.

I

We have met to-day to keep the festival of our Lord's Transfiguration. It is one of the lesser festivals ; and that not only with ourselves, but with the Church both in East and West. The great festivals of the Church commemorate the abiding work of the Lord, those great events of His life, those great experiences of His, which have made Him what He is to us to-day, and will be for ever. The Transfiguration was not one of these. It was an incident in the Apostles' training, a visible manifestation for a moment of the glory of their Lord, of His relation to those great servants of His purpose, whose work had been done before His day, of His relation above all to the Father, who had sent Him, and commanded that He should be heard and obeyed. But it was a revelation, which was not to last except in memory, and which was not to be proclaimed to others till the Son of Man had risen from the dead. Such an incident, however deep its interest and far-reaching its lessons, can never form part of the primary ground of the Church's faith, nor be proclaimed as a primary part of our message. It is an incident to be pondered quietly, as we ponder it this morning, by those already convinced of the Resurrection of the Lord. But for such it is surely most valuable. There is teaching in the fact that the revelation was given, and teaching also in the fact that it was withdrawn.

We look then at St. Mark's narrative, and what is it that we see ? We see that the great manifestation is given, not to create faith, but to reward faith, and encourage it in view of the dark days to come. The Transfiguration appears in close connection both with the confession of

St. Peter, and with the Lord's prophecy of His approaching
Passion. While the Lord had been leading the Apostles
to faith in His Messiahship, He had shown them little either
of His inherent glory, or of the path marked out for Him.
The Apostles had seen the Lord in His life among men,
known Him as the Teacher and the Healer, and as One
with a strange power, even over the world of nature. But
all this had given to them a problem rather than the
answer to it. "What manner of man is this, that even
the winds and the sea obey Him?" On the other hand,
the darker side of the future had been also hidden from
them. The Lord might have said nothing to encourage
their extravagant hopes of earthly glory, but He does not
at first seem to have set Himself to destroy them. If He
had spoken of His death, it had only been in veiled and
mysterious language which was not understood at the time.
But now that faith in His Messiahship is at last assured,
there is a change. Our Lord begins to speak in the clearest
words of His approaching rejection and death, and of the
necessity of all His followers taking up the Cross ; and, on
the other hand, the faith reached is rewarded, and encour-
aged in view of the future by this wonderful Transfiguration. That was surely most necessary. The victory that
faith had already won was no final victory. Faith had yet
to be tried by darker experiences than it had known
before, and the new revelation is given that faith may bear
the strain.

Very wonderfully is the revelation adapted to the
need. The time is coming when Jesus will be seen prostrate in the Garden, and uplifted on the Cross, and when
His vesture will be all stained with His blood. The time
is coming when all who claim to speak for the Law and
the Prophets will be arrayed against Him, when, instead
of overawing Kings and peoples with Moses and Elijah
of old, He will be the sport and contempt of them all.
The time is coming when even the Father will seem to
have forsaken Him who claimed to be His Son, and when
that Son will cry out in the darkness, and seem to find

M

no answer. How will faith persist in all this ? Do they
not need to see the Divine Glory shining out from the
Body and the very garments of the Lord ? Do they not
need to see Moses, who knew nothing of the Cross, and
Elijah, who, we can but think, might have repudiated it,
speaking with the Lord of the exodus He is to accomplish
at Jerusalem ? Do they not need that the Father Himself
should bear witness to the Lord, and be heard to claim
for Him their obedience ? Yes ! they need the vision, and
the vision is given. And yet, on the other hand, they do
not need that the vision should last. If, as St. Peter said,
it was good for them to be there, it was good for them also
to descend again to the trials and the tasks of the world.
God's work can no longer be done, as by Barak of old,
through a conquering host rushing down from Mount
Tabor ; it can be done no longer by fiery law and prophetic
judgment, and the presence of God manifest to outward
eye and ear. It must be done by "Jesus only with themselves"—by Jesus at work in His Body the Church,
and by the Church filled with His Spirit, and working by
His methods, bearing His Cross and dying, that it may
some day more abundantly live.

II

This then is the teaching of our Lord's Transfiguration.
Great revelations of the power and glory of our Lord are
given to us when we need them, and not before. We
must never demand them, we must never allow others to
demand them, in order that we may believe. We must
not ask for any sign from heaven ; it is an evil and adulterous
generation which asks for that ; it is the will of God that
in our lives for Him here we should walk by faith, and not
by sight. We must attend to the evidence that God has
given us of the glory of the Lord, to the witness of His
character and of His teaching, of His mighty works and
of His glorious Resurrection, to the witness of that standing
miracle, the existence of the Church, and to the witness borne

by the wonderful adaptation to our needs of the faith that
He has taught us. We must pray for the divine light, we
must purify our hearts that we may see God, and God will
enlighten us and our people to recognize the glory of His
Son. Then, when we see, we must act ; we must make
the plunge which faith demands, and not ask for further
light, when God has given us enough already. If it be
God's will that we should serve Him and work for Him
in the twilight, in the twilight we will serve and work.
Higher revelations will be given to us, if we need them,
after we have believed. God will not allow us to be
tempted more than we are able to bear—and if He knows
that we are to be greatly tried, He will give us the revelation that will prepare us for it.

> "One Christ for all, and fully Christ for each ;
>   So haply, as at Eucharist we knelt,
> Something that thrilled us more than touch or speech
>   Has made its presence felt :
> And round us draws a lucid atmosphere
>   Of self-commending truth, and love and might,
> And turned our faith from hearing of the ear
>   To sweet foretaste of sight."

It is so—is it not ?—at times, and most often, I think,
when we have been most cast down, and most stand in
need of it. Only we must remember that the vision that
comes must also go, and leave Jesus only with ourselves.
Our faith, like the faith of the Apostles, must be tried and
tested by suffering ; we must do our work as the Lord
did His.

But it is not of faith in our Lord in our own individual
lives that I want chiefly to speak to you to-day. It is of
faith in the Church, His Body, and of the future that lies
in store for her. If the Church is the Body of Christ, the
complement of Him who fills all in all, will not the revelation of her glory in this world be like the revelation of His,
a revelation which is the reward of our faith in her, and
the support of our faith in her, and yet a revelation that
seems at first to come only to raise hopes which in this
world are never realized ? It was so, I think, at the first ;

it is so, I think, still. Let me try to make my meaning clear.

How was it first in the early days of the Church of Christ? How gradually did the Apostles come to understand the true position of the Church, and the way in which she was to suffer and to fail! Read the early speeches of St. Peter in the Acts of the Apostles. How little the Passion in some ways seems to have taught him! He looks forward, it would seem, to just such an immediate triumph for the Church as he had before expected for the Lord. What he hopes for is a national conversion and an immediate return of the Lord. "And now, brethren, I wot that in ignorance ye did it, as did also your rulers. But the things which God foreshowed by the mouth of all the prophets, that His Christ should suffer, He thus fulfilled. Repent ye therefore, and turn again that your sins may be blotted out, that so there may come seasons of refreshing from the presence of the Lord. . . . Ye are the sons of the prophets, and of the covenant which God made with your fathers. . . . Unto you first God, having raised up His Servant, sent Him to bless you, in turning away every one of you from your iniquities." And, when later the hope of national conversion dies away, the outlook of the Apostles seems to widen rather than contract. "I would not, brethren, have you ignorant of this mystery . . . that a hardening in part hath befallen Israel, until the fulness of the Gentiles be come in ; and so all Israel shall be saved. . . . God hath shut up all the disobedience, that He might have mercy upon all." How strangely foreshortened is the Apostles' outlook upon the world! The Lord will come, they think, in their own day—it is a real difficulty to the mind when Christians die—and the Church will be glorified with Him.

Now we notice that at first the Holy Ghost no more destroys their illusions about the coming triumph of the Church than the Lord at first had destroyed their illusions about His own coming triumph. The truth must be learned through experience. First, the mission to the Jews failed. It was the election who obtained, and the rest were hardened. Then came the wide failure of the mission to the Gentiles. "All they in Asia have turned away from me." And now the Church begins to see, as the Lord had seen, that though the glory will come, the Passion must come first. There is no failure in faith. The Church is the Body of Christ, the Temple of the Living God, the pillar and ground of the Church. In her Divine Life the Church is indestructible. And yet before she can fully live, the Church must die. There in front of her is apostate Jerusalem, the great city, that spiritually is called Sodom and Egypt, where the Lord was crucified, the harlot city, that rests on the support of Rome, instead of that of God. There is that ravening wild beast, the Empire of Rome. There is the second beast, the False Prophet, the organized worship of the Empire. How will the Church fare now ? "Watchman, what of the night ? Watchman, what of the night ?" Ah ! the outlook is menacing now, "The morning cometh, and also the night." How will the Church fare in it ? And now, before the eyes of St. John comes the Transfiguration of the Church. James has fallen, and Peter has fallen, but John remains. And to him at Patmos the vision comes of the glory of the Church. Once more, he sees the Lord transfigured. "His head and his hair were white as white wool, white as snow ; and his eyes were as a flame of fire ; and his feet like unto burnished brass, as if it had been refined in a furnace ; and his voice as the voice of many waters." Yes ! but now not the Lord only is transfigured, but the Church as well. "And he carried me away in the Spirit to a mountain great and high, and showed me the holy city Jerusalem, coming down out of heaven from God, having the glory of God ; her light was like unto a stone most precious, as it were a jaspar stone, clear as crystal. . . . And the city hath no need of the sun, neither of the moon to shine upon it : for the glory of God did lighten it, and the lamp thereof is the Lamb." And once again, the two witnesses, Moses and Elijah, are seen bearing their witness,[*] leading the Church on the martyrs'

*Cf. Rev. xi., 3ff.

path, and once again the Voice of God bears witness to His own. "And I heard a great voice out of the throne saying, Behold, the tabernacle of God is with men, and He shall dwell with them, and they shall be His people, and God Himself shall be with them and be their God." So St. John writes what he has seen and the martyr-church is made strong to bear. Meanwhile she must purify herself, and go on with her witness. The glory will come, but the great tribulation must come first. "The vision is yet for the appointed time. . . . Though it tarry, wait for it."

III

My brothers, you see the message for ourselves to-day. If you and I have seen in some small measure the glory of the Church, it is to make us strong, and to make us patient. Do not let us be discouraged, because so few see it with us ; it was but three who went up to the mountain with our Lord. Do not let us fret, because we have to live and work with those who see it not ; the three who had seen went back to work with the nine who had not, and could not even tell them about it ; the rest will know, when the Church has risen from the dead. Do not let us be angry because those who see not do not act as those who see— how should it be otherwise ? Do not let us grow cold and bitter, because for awhile the vision we have seen may seem to fade, and the hopes we have built upon it not be realized. It came, that vision of the transfigured Church, in the early days of the Oxford movement. The Church, that so long had seemed but a human institution, was seen to glow with a supernatural glory. Her face did shine as the sun, and her garments became white as the light. Men thought of her as Moses, giving laws to the world, as Elijah withstanding kings, shutting up and opening the heavens in the name of God. For the moment all things seemed possible. What we had to do was to proclaim the Church, to make the world understand her apostolic succession and her divine authority, and England would be won to her. Very natural and very right were the illusions of those early days ; but they were illusions, and, if we have eyes to see, we know them now for what they were. Most true was the belief in the Church, upon which the hopes rested, but the hopes themselves, where are they ? The outward change that has passed over the face of the Church in England is very great ; it is due to many things beside the Oxford Movement ; but the inward change is surely not so great. The Oxford Movement has affected the minds of the few, not of the many. We have had our vision, but we have not made England see it with us. How do the great body of our people—the artisans and the labourers, the shopkeepers, the doctors, and the lawyers, the country gentry, and the men of affairs—how do they think of the Church ? For the most part, much as they thought of it before. What has affected them has been just what affected them before, and will always affect them, the loving sympathy of the parish priests, the heroic labours of the clergy in the slums, the work spoken in season, as they were able to hear it. High claims, high doctrines have gone for little ; it is the lives that have told. And if once more the Church seems to have been transfigured, if we have realized in a new way the greatness of that part of the Church which is in communion with ourselves, do not let us think that it will be otherwise with this vision than it has been with those which have gone before it. It is the few that have seen it, and the few that will act upon it.

> "The tumult and the shouting dies ;
> The captains and the kings depart."

What remains is "Jesus only with ourselves". And we turn and go down from the mountain to the plain below to find there the old dull throng, and the Church in her weakness, and the wise of this world questioning with her ; we go down to be content if we can soothe the world's pain, and find here and there a devil to be cast out by prayer. We go down, as of old, not to patent victory, but to seeming defeat ; we go down with our Master to suffer, and to die, if need be, for those to whom God has sent us.

SERMON XXV

PUBLICANS AND SINNERS

St. Matthew's Day

"As Jesus passed by from thence, he saw a man called Matthew, sitting at the place of toll : and he saith unto him, Follow me. And he arose, and followed him."— MATT. ix. 9.

WHAT a revelation of our Lord's spiritual power we have in to-day's Gospel ! Here is a man regarded as an outcast by his neighbours, and making his living under continual temptation to dishonesty ; and yet, the moment that our Lord calls, he is ready to answer, and give up all at His command. And how great has been the value to the Church of the victory which our Lord here won ! A few days or weeks, and St. Matthew was an Apostle ; a few years, and he was probably an evangelist, showing forth, in the beautiful words of to-day's epistle, "the light of the knowledge of the glory of God in the face of Jesus Christ." Scholars do not now as a rule believe that St. Matthew wrote the Gospel which is called by his name. But it is more than probable that St. Matthew—the one Apostle, as far as we know, accustomed to the pen—wrote down much of the teaching of the Lord, and that the Gospel "according to" St. Matthew reproduces his work more fully than any other Gospel does.

I

But it is not of St. Matthew himself that we will think this morning ; but of our Lord's wonderful success with the publicans and sinners of His day, in its contrast with our own failure to win those who now correspond to them.

Let me explain my meaning. The life and teaching of our Lord made a strong appeal, not only to the best people of his time, but to many of those who were regarded as the worst. Men and women who had lost touch with religion drew near to listen to Him, and in many cases were won by His words. Our own lives and teaching make no such appeal. I do not say that out lives and words are useless ; but their usefulness seems to be restricted to a small number of people. We interest and help those already in sympathy with us, but make little appeal to the world outside. The vast majority seldom enter our churches ; and, even when they do, seem not to be attracted by what they find there. How are English people divided to-day ? Almost everywhere we find a small body of people sincerely attached to the Church and making good use of their spiritual opportunities, and a larger body loosely attached, who worship with us now and again, but only rarely communicate. Finally, there are those outside who take no apparent interest in religion. But the great difference between the ancient and modern situation lies here. Among the Jews the publicans and sinners, who had lost touch with the national religion, seem to have been a comparatively small class ; while among ourselves those who have lost touch form the great majority of our fellow-countrymen. As an East London clergyman expressed it, we find, not ninety-nine sheep in the fold, and one wander-ing ; but rather one in the fold and ninety-nine wandering. Now the life and teaching of our Lord broke down these divisions, while our own do not. The Church in England to-day over wide areas is ministering, more or less success-fully, and in our Cathedrals at vast expense, to the needs of a small body of religious people. The publicans and sinners go their own way, and have no interest in our doings, while we in our turn too often appear to have no interest in theirs. It is painful to recognize this, and consider how our Lord must regard it ; but there is the fact. Let us this morning examine our Lord's method, in the hope that we may be led to a better fulfilment of His will.

II

Now, as we look at our Lord's method, the first thing that we notice is this. Though He came to seek and to save that which was lost, it is doubtful whether He specially addressed Himself to the publicans and sinners. Apparently He ignored these divisions of which I have spoken, and addressed Himself to all in much the same way. When He said, "I came not to call the righteous, but sinners," there was surely a touch of irony about His words. When our Lord came down to us, He did not find any righteous people ; like the Baptist, He found us all unrighteous ; He called us all to repentance, and proclaimed His gospel of forgiveness to us all. So too it was in His daily life among us. There too He refused to discriminate. He ate and drank with the Pharisees ; and He ate and drank with publicans and sinners. He would be the guest of anyone who invited Him, and with just as little appearance of condescension in one case as in another. Now here surely lay part of the source of His wide appeal. Here, for the first time, was a religious teacher who refused to draw a hard and fast line between the righteous and the wicked, a religious teacher who could see evil in a Pharisee and good in a publican, and was prepared to take men as He found them. He knew well why the publicans were publicans. It was because, as He explained in the most beautiful of His parables, they had come to be in want, and saw no other way of making a living. They might be worse than other men—in some ways probably they were—or they might be better. Our Lord could look on them with sympathy and hope. Listen to St. Matthew's fellow-publican Zacchæus, as he opens his heart to the Lord, "Behold, Lord, the half of my goods I give to the poor ; and if I have wrongfully exacted aught of any man, I restore it fourfold." To the Lord he could explain Himself. He might never go to the synagogue, or be allowed to go there, but there were few Pharisees who were half as generous, or who carried on their business in so honest a way. The Pharisees

saw in him only a son of perdition ; our Lord saw in him
"a son of Abraham"; and so our Lord could win him, while
they could not. Do not we, the clergy and laity of the
Church to-day, need far more of our Lord's largeness of
heart and readiness to see the best in those who are unlike
ourselves? Human character is too complex a thing for
our classifications ; few things perhaps are more misleading
than the number of our attendances at Church. There is
plenty of worldliness among ourselves ; there is far more of
nobility among those who seem to us to be irreligious than
we are always ready to believe. Englishmen are often
guilty of a kind of inverse hypocrisy ; they pretend to be
less religious than they are. If we assume that they have
no religion they will not undeceive us. We best appeal
to them, when we see the best in them, and credit them
with the desire to do right.

We pass to the second ground of our Lord's influence.
He appealed to men's hearts and consciences, by laying
stress in His teaching on the things whose importance
they could understand. It was there that the Scribes
failed both in teaching and in example. "Woe unto you,
Scribes and Pharisees, hypocrites ! for ye tithe mint and
anise and cummin, and have left undone the weightier
matters of the law, judgment and mercy and faith : but
these ye ought to have done, and not to have left the other
undone. Ye blind guides, which strain out the gnat, and
swallow the camel." You see our Lord's point. The
Pharisees had no sense of proportion. It is right to be
careful about little things ; to use our Lord's illustration,
if we see a gnat floating in our drink, we naturally take it
out. It is not in the least the fact that those who refuse
to be scrupulous in small matters of duty are all the more
faithful in great ones ; indeed the opposite is generally
true. But the Pharisees gave to tiny matters the place
which only belongs to the great moral issues of life, and
the consequence was that they made little appeal to the
outside world. It is of little use to appeal to anybody,
unless we have his conscience upon our side ; we must,

as to-day's epistle teaches us, "by the manifestation of the truth commend ourselves to every man's conscience in the sight of God." Our Lord always did this. The publicans and sinners might ridicule the minute rules of the scribes, and say that they had no time to bother about them, but they could not ridicule the Sermon on the Mount, or say that the parable of the Prodigal Son had no bearing upon their lives. It is this putting of "first things first" which our Lord recommends to us in to-day's Gospel. "Go ye," He says, "and learn what that meaneth. I will have mercy and not sacrifice." We must learn that, if our appeal is to be a wide one. What Hosea meant was that in the eyes of God outward religious observance was of no value, when divorced from the doing of God's will in the practical issues of life. If we wish to appeal to ordinary men and women, we must make them see that the Church mainly stands for justice between man and man, practical care for the weak and suffering, trust in God and obedience to God at any cost to ourselves, and not primarily for things whose value they do not yet appreciate. With English people the moral appeal generally goes home before the religious, since our moral instincts are relatively strong, and our religious instincts relatively weak. When men have come to care more as they should for justice, mercy, and faith, they will care more for Him, in whom they were all incarnate, and for those means of union with Him, which we need, if we are ever to become like Him. But the means of grace cannot rightly be put first, and, still less, tiny matters of religious practice. Too often to-day we seem to lay all the stress upon what the world is not as yet able to understand.

I have kept till the last the greatest sources of our Lord's appeal. They were His own character, and the splendour of the life to which He called us. Do we not often suppose that in order to appeal to men we must make ourselves as like them as we conscientiously can, and ask of them as little as may be ? The truth is the very opposite to this. The men and women of the world are attracted by the saints far more than by us ordinary Christians, and are often far more likely to aim at the saintly life than at our ordinary level of Christian practice. Have we not known high-spirited people, of whom the one thing certain was that they would never be ordinary Christians? They may aim at holiness, or they may be open sinners, but they are not likely to take an intermediate line. The reason for this is simple. It costs us all much to make any fundamental change in our lives, and we do not attempt it unless the change seems to us worth making. St. Matthew and Zacchaeus had no desire to resemble the Pharisees; if that had been the alternative, they would have gone on as they were. The life to which our Lord called them was a different matter. They did desire what He could offer them, and were prepared for sacrifice in order to obtain it. So it is to-day. The people of the world have very little desire to resemble us ordinary Christians. We seem to them, generally speaking, to be little better than themselves, though we make a hobby of religion. What is needed is a great improvement in our practice. Then, and not till then, shall we be able to make the sort of appeal that our Lord made.

III

One thing more. Will not the Gospel of St. Matthew help us here? It is not the gospel we shall use most in appealing to the outcast; the gospel for the outcast is undeniably St. Luke's. Nor is it the gospel we shall use most in our first appeal to any of those who have lost touch with religion. But it is the gospel for Christians who want to become more like our Lord, because it is the gospel which has preserved for us our Lord's moral teaching as no other has done. Shall we not show our gratitude to the Lord for St. Matthew's call by using his Gospel for the purpose for which it seems chiefly to have been given to us; to show us what the Lord intended the citizens of His Kingdom to be, in order that they might be the salt of the earth and the light of the world ? Most rightly do we tell men that there is no attaining to the likeness of Christ without the grace of Christ, but they see the difficulty of Christian holiness clearly enough without any telling. What they need to learn is rather that with the grace of Christ the likeness of Christ is attainable. That is what it is our task to show them.

THE GARMENT OF THE CHURCH

Conference of the Drapers' Association.

"The King's daughter is all glorious within ; her clothing is of wrought gold. She shall be brought unto the King in raiment of needlework ; the virgins that be her fellows shall bear her company, and shall be brought unto thee. With joy and gladness shall they be brought ; and shall enter into the King's palace."—Psa. xlv. 14-16 (P.B.V.).

There is, brethren, a distinction which we must often remember as we read the Old Testament. It is the distinction between the original meaning of the words and the meaning which they now have for us. In early days the Jews were accustomed to treat their literature very freely. They combined old materials in a new way ; they corrected and added to what they found ; and, as their knowledge of God increased, they put new and higher meanings upon old and familiar words. When the Christian Church took over the Old Testament from the Jews, it used a similar freedom. It did not, indeed, further alter the words which it found ; we read them to-day much as our Lord must have read them. But the fuller knowledge which the Church possessed enabled her teachers to find in the Old Testament a deeper meaning than even the Jews had found : and it is with this deeper meaning that we are chiefly concerned to-day. What the words originally meant often matters little ; what they mean as part of the Bible matters a great deal. The Bible is the Church's book ; we interpret it rightly when we interpret it in accordance with the Church's mind.

I

What then is the forty-fifth Psalm ?   It is a Psalm,
as the chapter-heading in our English Bible rightly says,
of "the majesty and grace of Christ's kingdom."   But it
does not appear to have been always this ; at first it was
a marriage song.   Some King ot Israel—Solomon perhaps,
or Ahab, or Jehoram—was taking into his harem a foreign
princess, and a court poet wrote a song for the occasion.
He begins, in the usual strain of Oriental compliment,
by praising the beauty and graciousness of the king, and
declaring that God's blessing will continually rest upon
him.   He then exhorts the king to attack his neighbours,
and draws with a few sharp strokes a picture of the over-
throw of the enemy.   Next, he turns to affairs at home.
Addressing the king, it would seem, as a divine being,
he praises the justice of his government, and explains by
it the happiness which God has bestowed upon him.

And now he comes to the main subject of his poem,
the royal wedding, if wedding it may be called.   Very
magnificent is the king—the poet praises, in passing, the
perfume of the royal garments, the decorations of the
royal palace, and the music of the royal band.   The king
has a large harem already, and already it contains daughters
of the neighbouring kings ; but the new wife is apparently
to be the queen-consort.   The poet points out to her what
she is to do.   She is to forget her own people and the
home of her childhood ; she is to accept the king as her
lord and master, and prostrate herself before him.   The
wedding presents will be splendid—especially from the
nobles, who hope to use the new queen's influence for
their own advantage.   And her majesty's clothes !   "The
king's daughter is all glorious within : her clothing is of
wrought gold."   By "within" the poet means within the
the palace.   That is where the queen-consort will be ;
she will hardly ever leave it, except to walk under strict
escort in the palace park.   But, if she and her ladies-in-
waiting enter the king's palace to be just as really his

slaves as those that sweep his stairs, the queen at any
rate will enjoy such satisfaction as cloth-of-gold and
embroidery are able to bestow.   The Psalm concludes
with the happy suggestion that the king shall carve out
kingdoms for his vast family from the nations he has
conquered.

There is the poem in its original meaning.   How do
we like it ? We will not blame the poet, for he knew no
better. But what kind of kings for foreign peoples would
the king's sons, born and bred in the harem, probably
have made ?   What do we think of the harem itself ?
The Oriental harem is one of the vilest institutions in
the world—horribly degrading to the poor women who
live in it, and still more horribly degrading to the man
who owns it, and prides himself upon it. He may think
that he has a multitude of wives, but in truth he has no
wife at all. The beautiful word "wife" is like the beautiful
word God ; it has no plural. Just as to have more gods
than one is to have no god worthy of the name, so to have
more wives than one is to have no wife worthy of the
name. No one can be a wife to a man who is not faithful
to her. If you want to see what a royal harem means—
not its sensuality only, but its jealousies, its intrigues, the
dreadful tragedies which it brings about—read the story
of King David's family life, the story of Michal and
Bathsheba, of Amnon and Absalom and Adonijah.   A
nice, happy home, was it not ?—so affectionate, so har-
monious, so restful, so much "joy and gladness" for everybody. If we are to judge the harem-system by its fruits,
it is not easy to find a more poisonous growth.

II

But now you will say : "If that is what the poem
means, what is it doing in the Bible ?" But that is not
what it means ; it is only what is meant ; before it found a
place in the Bible its meaning had been changed.   We
look forward some seven hundred years.   The Levites

N

in the temple are singing it, and there is a boy of twelve
years old listening to it, who has come up to Jerusalem for
His first Passover. What do they care for its original
meaning? Kings of the Jews there are now no longer.
But there is a King to come, the Christ of God, the great
instrument of God to redeem His people, and rule them
in mercy and truth. "Fairer" He will be "than the children
of men", and "full of grace" His "lips" ; He will "reign
over the house of Jacob for ever", and "of His Kingdom
there will be no end". And as the Levite choir sings,
and the boy listens to the song, it is of this King that they
think, and of Him alone.

And the Queen, the King's daughter—who is she?
The Queen is Israel, the Church and people of God, in
her devotion to God and the Christ Whom He will send.
One day the boy will speak of Himself as "the bridegroom",
and of His union with His people as a wedding feast.
Strange, is it not? How did they come so to interpret
the Psalm? Let us see. The people of God had come to
know far more of marriage than court poets could teach
them, for they were no longer polygamists. If the shepherd
in his upland cot, or the workman in the bazaar, could
support one wife, he did very well. The wife and mother
in Israel had something better to do than to knock her
forehead on the ground before her lord and master. She
had her children to wash and clothe, and her man's supper
to prepare ; and, if she missed a coin from her little store,
she had to light a candle in her dark little house, and
sweep diligently till she found it. And so, though I fear
she wore no cloth-of-gold, there could be love in her
home, and mutual respect ; and she and her man could
come to know what God meant married life to be. And
that led them further. They could understand what the
great prophets meant, when they said that the love of
God for His people was like the love of a husband for his
wife, and that the love of God's people for Him ought
to be like the love of a wife for her husband ; and that,
if they wished to understand the agony of God when His

people were unfaithful to Him, they were to think of
the agony of a loving and faithful husband when his wife
proved unfaithful.

And so wonderfully, I think, did these thoughts take
hold of the people of God, that they read a new meaning
into the love-songs of their literature. The Rabbis hesi-
tated long before they admitted the Song of Songs into
the Old Testament. If they did admit it at last, it was,
I think, because they had come to put this new spiritual
meaning upon it, to interpret it of the love of God for His
people, and of His people for Him.

So too with the forty-fifth Psalm. Its meaning at
the court of Israel long ago was one thing, but its meaning
in the Bible is another. The Church, in taking over from
the Jews the Song of Songs and the forty-fifth Psalm,
took them over in their higher meaning. To the Church
the lover in the Song of Songs, and the bridegroom in
the Psalm, are always the Lord Christ—at once God,
whose throne "endures for ever", and man, fairer than the
children of men, who here loved righteousness and hated
iniquity, and whom God in the world unseen has anointed
with the oil of gladness above His fellows ; and the Queen
is the Church or people of God, and you and I its members.

And as, remembering this, you read the Psalm, you
will find that almost every verse is taking to itself a new
and beautiful meaning. The sword becomes the sword of
the Spirit, which is the Word of God, the divine message
spoken by our Lord's lips, and the sharp arrows in the
hearts of His enemies the shafts of His love turning them
into His friends ; and the fragrant vestments remind
us of the human body which He wore, ever redolent to
our thoughts of myrrh, aloes and cassia, because of the
spices in which it was wrapped when it lay in the ivory
palace of Joseph's rock-hewn tomb. And if, being English
people and not so imaginative as the Fathers of the Church,
we complain that this is "really too much", and ask for
something practical, the Psalm rightly interpreted will
supply it. For we shall see that, when it calls us for our

Lord's sake to forget our own people and our father's house, it says to us only what the Lord Himself said : "He that loveth father or mother more than Me is not worthy of Me, and he that loveth son or daughter more than Me is not worthy of Me," and we shall learn to put His will for us before the will of any other, however dear.

So, brethren, let us learn to use, not only this Psalm, but the Song of Songs and much else in the Old Testament ; and, when the modern commentator has taught us what once they meant, go to St. Bernard and the other Fathers to learn what they mean.

III

Is there anything else ? Well ! I must not be silent about the Queen's garments. There is a philosophy of clothes, as Thomas Carlyle has taught us ; and, if we know how people like to be dressed, we know something about the people themselves. How is it with the people of God ? What says the New Testament ? It tells us that the only wear for the people of God is "the righteous acts of the saints", those good works which God has afore prepared that we should walk in them, and which are the expression of the Divine life within. We must have the heart right first : "the king's daughter is all glorious within". But the heart is not enough ; garments must be seen ; out of the abundance of the heart the mouth must speak and the hand must act, if we are to stand at least at the King's right hand "in a vesture of gold, wrought about with divers colours."

And if we ask why the Queen must be brought to the King "in raiment of needlework", the answer is that the Christian character is never machine-made. It has to be formed, day by day, through a multitude of tiny actions, each right in its time and place—little unseen strivings after perfect purity, and perfect honesty, and perfect truth—"little, nameless, unremembered acts of mercy and of love". It is tedious, no doubt ; needlework is always that, especially if we drop our stitches ; but there is nothing like it for beauty, and nothing like it for wear, and nothing like it for the glory which it gives to God and the influence which it exercises over men.   It is when the Queen is brought unto the King in raiment of needlework, that the virgins that be her fellows bear her company and are brought with her.   And what that says to us is that if the man in his office and the girl in her warehouse would exercise a strong influence for good upon those with whom they live, they must be Christians, not some of the time, but all the time, and remember that everything they say and do has its own importance.   So may we all with joy and gladness be brought and enter into the King's palace. So may Christ our Lord "instead of" His "fathers have children", not only the old to serve Him, but the young also, and His Kingdom be extended among all the peoples of the earth.

Sermon XXVII

INGRATITUDE

Harvest Festival

"And Jesus answering said, Were not the ten cleansed, but where are the nine? Were there none found that returned to give glory to God, save this stranger."—Luke xvii. 17, 18.

WE hear in these words a profound disappointment. It was not our Lord's way to make much of injuries done to Himself, nor does He do so here: what troubles Him is the ingratitude to God, whose agent He was, and to whose restoring power the cure of the lepers was due. True—the Lord had told the lepers to go and show themselves to the priests; and they were doing as He told them. There they are, disappearing in the distance on the road to Jerusalem. But might they not have come back first to offer their thanksgiving? The Samaritan did, though no doubt he went to his priest afterwards. But the Jews— no. Faith they had, or there would have been no healing; obedience they had, as we have seen. But gratitude to God, or to the Lord His Minister? There is no sign of that. There is none found returning to give glory to God save the stranger from Samaria.

I

We have met to-day for our Harvest Festival, our Harvest Thanksgiving. Which title most accurately describes our spirit? The word festival suggests personal rejoicing—we are all glad of the harvest. The word thanksgiving points us to God Himself—are we all thankful

for it ? My brothers, do you find it easy to be rightly
thankful for God's earthly gifts—not glad only, but
thankful ? I find it very difficult ; perhaps you do also.
We know that from God comes all that we enjoy ; we
have nothing, as St. Paul says, that we have not received.
Food and clothing and shelter ; peaceful homes and
healthful days ; the beauty of earth and sea and sky ;
science and art, and music, and sport ; our pleasant inter-
course with our neighbours, the love of our friends and
of our families—do these things so fill us with thankful-
ness, that the love of God and the desire to please Him
grow ever stronger as we think of them, and we feel that
we must ever be returning to give Him thanks ? I find
myself most ungrateful ; perhaps you do also.

And yet—are we quite as bad as we seem ? Suppose
that a neighbour of ours goes out of his way to do us a
personal kindness, to which we do not see that we have
any claim. We respond instantly—do we not ?—and so
do others to us. Why then are we so ungrateful to God ?
It is very strange ; there must be a mistake somewhere ;
shall we try to-day to get to the bottom of it ? If we find
the cause, we may also find the remedy ; and what a
blessing it will be if we do ! "It is a good thing to give
thanks unto the Lord, to sing praises unto Thy Name,
O Most Highest." Yes ! it is good—good in itself, and
good in the glory it gives to God, and good for us too.
For, though there may be many happy people who are
not thankful, there are no thankful people who are not
happy.

II

We begin then our investigation of ingratitude ; and here
in the Gospel are nine patients suffering from the disease.
We shall not blame them prematurely ; we shall adopt
the better method, and try to understand them first.
Why did those nine Jews not come back to give thanks,
while the one Samaritan did ?

We observe that our Lord was at this time on His way

to Jerusalem. His ministry was drawing to a close, and
He was going up to die. By this time, I suppose, our
Lord's healing power had lost its novelty ; everyone took
it for granted that He would heal the sick, and the nine
Jews expected to be healed. Jesus of Nazareth was their
own prophet, sent by God to the lost sheep of the house
of Israel, and to no one else. If the Lord healed them,
it did not seem to prove any special regard for them,
or special pity for them ; it was just what He always did,
and was there to do. With the Samaritan it was otherwise ;
he never expected to be healed. Jesus was to him the
prophet of an alien and hostile people ; if He came near
to Samaria, it was only because He was journeying to
Jerusalem. The Samaritan leper lifted up his voice for
pity like the rest, but he expects no answer ; and when
the answer comes, he finds it overwhelming. This Jesus
is quite unlike all other Jews ; He cares for the Samaritan,
and has given him this wonderful and unexpected blessing.
Gratitude, you see, is a personal matter : what calls it
out is not so much the greatness of the blessing, as the
open hand that gives it, and the generous heart that opens
the hand. What comes to us without the touch of personal
good will never move us ; windfalls are all to the good,
but we do not thank the wind. It is the love that we
care for even more than the gift ; and

> Rich gifts wax poor when givers prove unkind.

Have we got to the bottom of our ingratitude ? I think
that in part we have. The reason why we thank God
so little for our earthly blessings is that we do not see
in them any sign of His individual love. We believe in
God, and we believe that from Him all good things come ;
we recognize in some degree His goodness in them all.
We see that His world not only provides for our needs,
but for our pleasure also. How precious are the fields of
standing corn, but also how beautiful ! Nature, it has been
well said, while it works as a machine, sleeps as a picture.
The harvest is necessary to keep us alive ; but why should

the corn as it ripens be not only useful, but lovely too ?
But is there in all this anything personal to ourselves ?
It does not seem so. God gives to us, we suppose, because
He gives to all ; but "what are our souls in a boundless
creation" ? The universal Father does not think of you
or me. It is with Him, we think, as with a rich man who
sets himself to benefit his native city. He loves the place
where he has prospered, and delights in benefitting its
people ; the park, and the free library, and the art-gallery,
and the local university, are the expression of his living
goodwill. But, though he cares for all, he cannot care
for each ; and so the gratitude which he awakens, however
real, is not of an individual and personal kind. The father
of a family, in planning a treat for his children, may think
of the pleasure of each one ; he may hang presents upon
the Christmas tree chosen with special thought for each
one of his children, but the city philanthropist cannot
do that ; his munificence is munificence to the city, and
it is enough if the Mayor and Corporation, in accepting
his gifts, send him a grateful letter for them. And so,
we suppose, it is with God. At an Harvest Thanksgiving
we will take our share in the hymns of praise, but God's
generosity does not come personally home to ourselves,
so we are not really grateful.

My brothers, do you know what we are doing ? We are
confusing the mind of God with the mind of man. May I
ask your careful attention to this : it is not quite easy to
explain, but it is very important.

Observe then that our human minds have to use as
their instruments our human brains ; and we are so made
that we can never attend to more than one thing or person
at a time. I may seem to write a letter while I carry
on a conversation, but in fact I only turn alternately
to the one and to the other ; I cannot really write the
simplest letter while I am attending to something else.
So again I cannot think of a whole and of its parts at the
same time. The thing to which I am attending may be
large, and complicated—a machine, or a family, or a

nation, or the world. But if I think of the whole, I cannot at the same time think of the parts, though my mind may move rapidly from the one to the other. In a similar way, if I think of a part, I cannot at the same time think of the whole to which it belongs, and that means that I understand the part only most imperfectly. For everything is what it is by its relations with its surroundings, and the larger wholes to which it belongs; to understand any one thing perfectly, we should have to understand the universe.

> Flower in the crannied wall,
> I pluck you out of the crannies;
> I hold you here, little flower, in my hand;
>   But if I could only understand
> What you are, root and all, and all in all,
> I should know what God and man is.

But can we apply such human limitations as these to God, whose "understanding is infinite"? Of course not. How could this wonderful world go on, unless both the whole, and each tiniest part were equally present to His mind? God sees the parts in the whole—each of us, not as a solitary unit, but in relation to all through which we are what we are. God sees the whole in the parts. If God so loved the world that He sent His Son to live and die for it, the world was nothing to Him apart from those individual men and women who have the highest place in His purpose, and His love was a love for them as individuals and not merely in the mass. And so, when God bestows His blessings, He bestows them, not like the city philanthropist, who does not think of individuals, but like the father of a family who does. He knows with an intimate and personal knowledge every one of us who will profit by them or enjoy them, and intends that very profit and that very pleasure which each one actually receives. That God's blessings come to us again and again, the same blessings a thousand times; that they are for others as well as for you and me; does not affect in the slightest degree the fact that they come as directly from His Hand to you and to me as individual men and women, as if they were given only once, and no one enjoyed them but ourselves.

Indeed all blessing is and must be individual blessing, though it may spread in ever widening circles to the confines of the world. What do we mean when we say that we enjoy ourselves? We mean that all enjoyment is personal, and is only possible because we are as God has made us. We stand on the cliff on some clear September evening, as the setting sun picks out all the varied colour of the scene, and the blue of the sea deepens as the shadows fall. Do I see what you see, or do you see what I see? Not exactly. The perception is an individual perception. Each, in enjoying the prospect, is really enjoying his own particular perception, or enjoying himself. Our own particular pleasure is known only to ourselves and to Him Who has made us and gives it to us, knowing what He does, and rejoicing in and with us, as no one else can do. What said our Lord about the sunshine? Did He say that the sun shone? No, He said that God makes His sun to shine upon the evil and upon the good. It is His sun, and He Himself makes it to shine. As its rays fall upon the evil and the good, and on you and me, in whom there is so much of both, they come to each one of us straight from Him Who knows what each one is, and deliberately sends them none the less. I do not think we shall be unthankful if we remember what God's knowledge is, and the personal goodwill and deliberate intention with which His blessings come.

Sermon XXVIII

SILENCE

Sunday After Armistice Day

"And when Jesus came into the ruler's house, and saw the flute-players, and the crowd making a tumult, he said, Give place : for the damsel is not dead, but sleepeth."— Matt. ix. 23, 24.

So it must ever be, if real work is to be done. Some are able to be silent without too much distress, and some are not. Those who possess the gift must use it ; the rest must go outside. God's greatest works are done in silence.

I

We will think then this morning of silence. It is a thing both very valuable and very much neglected. Here on Armistice Day for two minutes we enjoyed it ; and we heard perhaps something better worth hearing than most that we hear. But two minutes are not much to give to so good a thing ; if we were silent oftener, we might hear much more. That is always the purpose of silence—not that we should repress our desire to speak for the sake of repressing it, but that we should be able to listen. Speech is silver, the old proverb says, but silence is golden ; and it may open to us treasures of greater price than gold. For observe that noise narrows the field of our attention by forcing it to concentrate upon that which is close at hand. We desire to work or to sleep. But no—there is a door banging in the distance, and we know that it will bang again ; or there are drops of water falling at regular intervals, and somehow we cannot take our attention away from them. So it is also with less unwelcome sounds, with music or the conversation of our friends. They too confine our attention to that tiny fragment of the world which is close at hand ; and if we never enter into silence, the range of our outlook will be narrow indeed. But, as silence falls, the world expands in time and space. The past and the future find themselves on more equal terms with the present. We can think, not only of the passing show, but of our city, our country, and the great world beyond. Indeed we may become conscious of another world than this ; of God, in Whom we live and move and have our being ; of the "peace-parted souls" of those who have gone before us, the great cloud of witnesses to the power of faith, whose approval is better worth having than any than we find here ; and, most clearly of all of ourselves who ought to be in time with them all, and yet are too often restless and unhappy, cabined and confined in a noisy and vulgar "here" from which escape seems impossible. How important then it is that we should often be alone and silent ! How great a mistake it is to fill up every moment of the day ! Dislike of silence is sometimes like a child's dislike of the dark ; it springs from fear of the unfamiliar and unknown. There is a story that the poet Southey was once speaking to a member of the Society of Friends. He explained, not without a touch of self-satisfaction, how he mapped out his time : so many hours for sleep, so many for reading, so many for writing, and so many for conversation. But his companion remained unimpressed. "Friend," he said, "when dost thou think ?"

II

Consider first the value of silence, that we may listen to others. Many of us have so much to say that we are bad listeners. "Be swift to hear," says the Son of Sirach ; "and with patience make thine answer. If thou hast understanding, answer thy neighbour ; and if not, let thine hand be upon thy mouth." Let us think of this for a moment. About all great subjects—politics, and morals, and religion—we should think for ourselves ; a faith which has cost us little is of little value. Moreover when the right time comes, it is right to say what we think, and make what contribution we may to the common stock of ideas. The young are often readier to speak than those who are older, and we should not wish to silence them. If they think themselves cleverer than the middle-aged and the old, they may be right in thinking this ; psychological tests prove, I understand, that at the age at which Freshmen usually come to Oxford their minds are quicker than they have ever been before, or ever will be again. But they should remember that the value of our opinions depends, not merely upon our quickness of mind, but upon the amount of information which we possess. All great subjects are difficult subjects ; and, if our knowledge is slight, we cannot have much that is of value to say. Thus, the Son of Sirach says again : "A wise man will be silent till his time come." The important thing at first is to acquire information, and silently to think about it and digest it. We should not as a rule speak much about it, until it has been digested, and it has forced its place in the previous content of our minds.

Consider secondly the silence that is necessary for the knowledge of ourselves—of our characters, our gifts, and the temptations which they bring. Silence is revealing. We read in the gospels that when our Lord was called to His work, the Spirit led Him into the wilderness. Why was this ? Was it to be alone with God ? The Gospels rather suggest that it was to be alone with the devil. In solitude it may take time to find God, but there is no shyness about the devil. He comes uninvited ; and the wilderness is the best place in which to meet him. So the Lord found. The temptations which were bound to come to Him all through His ministry, just because His gifts and calling were what they were, came to Him in the wilderness first. There He recognized them for what they were, and found the right answer to them ; He was forewarned

and so forearmed. So with ourselves. Tempted we must
be all through our lives, and each by temptations in part
peculiar to himself. When shall we meet them first ? In
the rush of life, where they are upon us before we have
time to think ; or in the silence, where we can observe
and come to know ourselves, recognize our weak points,
and deal with temptation in advance ? Why is it that
we often understand others so much better than ourselves ? It is because we observe others more than we
observe ourselves. Try the experiment of silence. Let
thoughts, memories, longings, castles in Spain, come just
as they will ; and observe them as they come. The things
which are dominating our outward action dominate also
our inner life. Perhaps it will be some old grievance that
will rise to the surface, or some habitual and urgent
desire. We shall see whither we are tending, and where
the point of danger lies. If you see that the course which
suggests itself is evil, do as the Lord did ; recognize for
your future guidance the principle that condemns it.
Once more let us hear the Son of Sirach. "A man's soul
is sometimes wont to bring him tidings, more than seven
watchmen that sit on high on a watch-tower." But watch-
towers should be silent places. If the seven watchmen
never cease talking, watching will be at a discount. It
is the same with the soul. It is only if it watches that it
can bring us tidings of any value.

Once more consider the value of silence, that we may
think of God, and that God may reveal Himself to us.
We must, as the Psalmist says, "be silent to the Lord,
and wait patiently for Him." There can be no conversation,
and no friendship, if the speech is always ours and never
God's. Sometimes through illness God makes the silence,
as our Lord made it in the text : but generally we must
make it for ourselves. "Enter into thine inner chamber,"
our Lord said, "and shut thy door." When we have done
so, we should listen to Him as well as speak to Him. Is
not the failure of much of our prayer due to the fact that
we make too little use of silence ? In our service to-day,

the sound of our voices has never ceased for a moment. If Christ Himself is in the midst of those gathered in His name, do we not need a little time to remember it and to listen to Him ? But we need not make the same mistake in our private prayers. I have heard it said that, even when we have but a short time for prayer, we should use half of it in being silent before God ; we need silence before we speak to Him, and silence afterwards. When the Lord went out to pray "a great while before day", and when He "continued all night in prayer to God", I do not think that His lips moved all the while, but that He listened as well as spoke. Should not we do the same ?

There is in the Revelation of St. John a wonderful phrase, which perhaps we may not have noticed. "There was silence in heaven." Look on, and you may see why. Beneath the heavenly altar are the souls of the martyrs, and there are others suffering in the great tribulation below. The prayers of all God's saints, living and departed, are going up fragrant with incense to His throne ; and so angels and archangels must be silent, lest the prayer should not be heard. If God makes a silence to listen to us, should not we make one to listen to Him ? There was no healing for Jairus's daughter, till the Lord's voice could be heard ; nor will there be healing for us either. We English Christians do not like silence or solitude ; and that is one reason why our religion is so shallow. It is well for almost all sometimes to go into Retreat ; it is being made far easier, even for the poor, than it used to be. But, if that is not possible, we can make Retreats of our own in church or at home, or out of doors under the open sky. God is always near ; but we may need silence, if we are to find Him. Like Jairus's little daughter, we are not dead, but only sleeping ; and though silence may suggest sleep rather than waking, it has sometimes the opposite effect. I have heard of people who lived close to a great railway junction, and who, when a railway strike occurred, found themselves much more awake at night than was usual with them.

Sermon XXIX

THE HOUSE OF GOD

Dedication Festival

"And Jacob rose up early in the morning, and took the stone that he had put under his head, and set it up for a pillar, and poured oil upon the top of it. And he called the name of that place Beth-el (that is, the house of God)."
—Gen. xxviii, 18, 19.

Here, in this old-world story, we find the first mention of the house of God. It was a humble beginning—just a stone set up as a pillar, and consecrated with oil. But there is a desire for drawing near to God and for communion with Him ; and God will lead us to better things in time.

I

Now the Bible is the record of a revelation of God : it begins low, but it ends high. God, if I may so say, stooped to conquer us ; He took us as we were that He might slowly make us what He desired us to be. Never therefore be surprised if you find here and there in the Bible low thoughts of God and of men. They are not the thoughts of God, but the thoughts from which His revelation came to deliver us. In thought, as well as in practice, we must ever rise "on stepping-stones" of our "dead selves to higher things".

Consider this story of Jacob. Scholars tell us that some of the oldest stories of Israel, like some of the oldest stories of England, were stories told at the ancient sanctuaries. This story of Jacob seems to come for the most part from the Northern Kingdom of Israel, and to have been told at the sanctuary of Bethel, where in after days the prophecy of Amos was delivered. Suppose that we had gone to Bethel in the days of the Judges or of the Kings.

What should we have seen there ? On the high ground outside the city, and under the open sky, we should have seen a rough altar, and behind it a large stone set up pillar-wise like the stones we may see at Avebury or Stonehenge. And, if we had asked the priest about the origin of the shrine, he would have told us, I think, something like this. Long ago Father Jacob passed by on his journey. He lay down to sleep with a stone for his pillow ; he dreamed that he saw a ladder set up between heaven and earth ; and then God revealed Himself to him. So, when he awoke in the morning, he knew that unaware he had stumbled upon holy ground. He took the stone that he had used as his pillow, set it up, and poured upon it the consecrating oil to make it the house of God ; and there, the priest would have said, is the stone to testify to the fact. God is in the holy stone. Bow down and worship Him here. Here bring your sacrifice ; and pay your tithe to the priest of Bethel, as Father Jacob paid his of old.

But then, we complain, this is grovelling superstition. How can God be confined in a stone ? Was the stone of Bethel any better than the meteoric stone that in St. Paul's day was worshipped as Diana of the Ephesians, or than the black stone of Mecca which the Muhammadans venerate still ? No better perhaps ; but if God is to raise us, He must find us where we are. And religion is really beginning. God makes to Jacob a promise ; and Jacob believes it, and bases his life upon it. And since Jacob means to live in dependence upon God, he desires to know where to find him. What place could be better than the place where He has already been found ? Suppose that in this church you first found God, and God first found you. Suppose that here and nowhere else you first learned that heaven is not far away ; but that, in Christ our Lord, God has set up a ladder from earth to heaven. Would you not love its very stones ? Would the greatest Cathedral in the world be to you quite what this church would be ? Would you not love to pray here, and here to make your offerings ; and, if you wandered far to other parts of the world, would you not wish some day to return and pray here again ? Sentiment ? Yes, but right sentiment. Who made us with hearts as well as heads ?

II

And now from Jacob let us pass to Solomon, and to those chapters, the fifth to the ninth of the First Book of Kings, which describe the building of the Temple. There is no time for details to-day ; you must read those chapters for yourselves ; but this is what you will find. There has been real progress in the thoughts of God's people ; we hear nothing at Jerusalem of holy stones ; but the desire of God's people for His presence with them is as strong as ever. That was the purpose of the temple—to provide for God a house worthy of Him, that so He might dwell among His people, and His saving power be available for them. That is why for seven years the temple was in building ; that is why Solomon hewed the cedars and shaped the stones ; that is why he provided "gold for the things of gold and silver for the things of silver." He thought that God's house "must be exceeding magnifical, of fame and glory throughout all countries." He would not dwell in a palace himself, and then provide a white-washed barn for God. Did he think that God could be confined in a temple, if not in a stone ? Not so. Listen to him as he speaks to God. "Behold, heaven and the heaven of heavens cannot contain thee ; how much less this house that I have builded !" But he did not think that God must be everywhere equally present. Our God is a living personal God, and His saving presence depends upon His will. If He willed to choose one city above all others, and one spot in that city above all others, to "place His Name there", and to promise that there His eyes and His heart would ever be open to those who called upon Him, who will say that He could not do so ? Jacob thought that God's presence was in some way tied to Bethel; Solomon thought that God's presence could be given where God willed, and prayed that it might be given in the house built for Him. So in that most moving prayer of Solomon there passed before him all the varied needs of men; the poor and oppressed crying for justice between man and man, the beaten and discouraged armies of Israel crying for the restoration of national freedom, the starving crying for food in the drought, the exiles in foreign lands homesick for the fields where they played as children, the individual Israelite with his individual sorrow; and he prays that all alike, as they turn to that inner shrine of the temple where God dwells, may find Him ready to hear them. "Hearken Thou to the supplication of Thy servant, and of Thy people Israel, when they shall pray toward this place: yea, hear them in heaven Thy dwelling place; and when Thou hearest, forgive."

Is that superstition? Is it not rather the religion of the Old Testament at its noblest? Let us take heed lest, instead of rising above it, we fall below it—below it in generosity and self-sacrifice for God, below it in our thoughts of God Himself. May I ask your attention to this? It is not quite easy to understand, but it is very important.

How, my brothers, do you and I think of God and of His presence with us? Do we think of Him as living, and personal, and free; or do we think of Him as if He were an all-pervading atmosphere? There are many who think of Him in the second way. God, they would say, is omnipresent and eternal. He cannot be more with us in one place than in another. He is as near us on the shore as He is in the church, as present at our breakfast-tables as at the Holy Communion itself. "In Him we live and move and have our being." To think otherwise is superstition like that of Jacob himself. Now will you forgive me if I put strongly what I am going to say? To think of God in that way is to think of Him in a way far more unworthy than that of Solomon, or of Jacob.

It is not to believe that God is everywhere, but that a little of Him is everywhere—too little for our reverence, and too little for our trust. It is to think of Him not as living, and personal, and free, but as present only because He cannot be absent. If we try to think of God, we must employ the highest conceptions that we have ; and our highest conceptions are those of personality and life. No doubt, the personality of God cannot exactly resemble ours ; it must be free from the limitations which are attached to ours. But, even though we think of God as more like ourselves than He can really be, we shall be far nearer the truth than if we think of Him, not as like something higher than ourselves, but as like something immeasurably lower.

Now how does the thought of God as living, and personal, and free, lead us to think of His presence ? God's presence depends upon His will. He is present as He wills and where He wills ; and in the ever-varying modes which His purpose requires. He is present in one way in the world, and in another in history ; He is present in one way in Christ, and in another by the Spirit in the Church of Christ. He is present wherever He "puts His Name", wherever He manifests Himself to us, and deals with our personal needs. God, it is true, is omnipresent and eternal, but you and I are neither. We are creatures of time and space, "here to-day, and gone to-morrow", and here, not elsewhere, while we are here. If God is to deal with us, He must deal with us under the actual conditions of our lives. He must come to us, as George MacDonald said of the baby, "out of the everywhere into here" ; He must Himself plunge into that "ever-rolling stream" of time, which "bears all its sons away". If He blesses, He must bless at some time and at some place ; and all the better for us if He appoints definite means for the manifestation of His saving power, and definite times for seeking it. So it is that the religion of the Bible and of the Church is always what we call "institutional religion" —a religion which tells us when, where, and how, to seek

God, and so enables us to find Him. Suppose that we put
all this aside as superstition. What will happen? We
may have a very lofty idea of God, or think that we have
it: but of God Himself we shall know little or nothing.
We may rise above holy stones, but not above our needs
as men and women; and, had we to choose between
Jacob's view of God, and the view so popular to-day,
we should choose Jacob's as the higher of the two.

III

And now from Jacob and Solomon we pass to our Lord.
What did He think about the house of God? He called
the temple His Father's house; He cast out those who
polluted it, and would not suffer it to be used just as a
thoroughfare. But He knew that it must pass away,
and He provided for us a better house of God than that.
"Destroy this temple," He said, "and in three days I
will raise it up"; and St. John tells us that He "spake
of the temple of His body". In Christ God was present
as never before and as nowhere else. In Christ He came,
as never before, "out of the everywhere into here," the
"here" of the stable of Bethlehem and of the Cross of
Calvary. The body of Christ born, growing, labouring,
suffering, dying, risen and ascended, was the one worthy
temple that God found among us; and though, as David
said, the house of God "must be exceeding magnifical, of
fame and glory throughout all countries", it is not marble
and gold that are longest remembered, but the beauty of
a human character, and the love of a human heart. It
was in Christ our Lord that God revealed Himself to us; and,
if we do not find Him there, we shall find Him nowhere else.
Finally, what of ourselves? God has sent down the
Spirit to bring the presence of Christ, and so of God, to us.
"Know ye not that ye are the temple of God, and that
the Spirit of God dwelleth in you." We are the true house
of God, and his manifestation and work must be carried
on through you and me. How the great medieval builders

taught us this! Look at one of our great cathedrals. The ground plan with its choir and nave and transepts is the body of Christ nailed to the Cross. The choir represents His head, and the transepts His outstretched arms; and sometimes—as at Stratford-on-Avon and Stamford St. Mary—the choir is not quite straight with the nave, but bent a little to the left, to remind us how He "bowed His head and gave up the ghost." Thus, when the building rises, it rests upon the body of Christ sacrificed for us; and the building is the people of God themselves. The pillars of the nave stand for the Apostles, and the bays of the choir for the orders of the angels, while the walls in some Oxford Colleges are covered by tiers of saints rising to the roof, and the light comes to us through the saints who fill the windows. So, as we take our places there, we know that we are "no more strangers and sojourners, but fellow-citizens with the saints and of the household of God, builded together for a habitation of God by the Spirit."

"Is it then," you will say, "wrong to call our church the house of God?" I should not quite say that. Rather I should say, in our homely phrase, that "it all depends". Suppose that you leave the church empty. Suppose that on wet days, you find it too wet for going to church, and on fine days too fine for anything but a country walk. Is it then much more than a material building? Is God really present there more than in the roads by which we reach it? But suppose that you remember what you are called to be, the living stones of the house of God. Suppose that you provide "gold for the things of gold" by freeing yourselves through the grace of God from all that prevents your lives from shining, and then fill your church from end to end. Then, just because you have brought God with you, the church, your house, is God's house too. Shall it not be so indeed in the days to come? Then we shall unite all that is best in the Old Testament teaching with the higher revelation brought by the Lord Himself. We shall build a house worthy to be the dwelling-place of God, a house in which He will dwell for ever.

Sermon XXX

THE TRANSCENDENCE OF GOD

College Festival

"Let God arise."—Psa. lxviii. 1.

That is our Ely battle-cry, the battle-cry all down the ages
of the Church of God. God must arise, and deal with the
situation ; no human power can grapple with it. "O God,
wonderful art Thou in Thy holy places, even the God of
Israel ; He will give strength and power unto His people ;
blessed be God."

I

It is a wonderful Psalm which we sang this morning.
We sang it, I hope, with our spirits ; but perhaps not all
with our understandings also. For the Psalm is difficult ;
and, like Ely Cathedral, it was not built in a day. God's
revelation of Himself has been a gradual revelation ; and,
though His people trusted and praised Him from the first,
they did not at first rightly understand His ways. Thus, as
their knowledge grew, they seem to have altered and
adapted their old songs of praise, and put new meanings
into them. Moreover, when the Lord had risen and the
Spirit had been given, the Psalms received a further transformation. Christians translated them ; and, their Christian
faith being stronger than their Hebrew scholarship, they
often in the happiest way read the new faith into the old
words. Study this sixty-eighth Psalm for yourselves, both
in the Revised and in the Prayer Book versions, and see
how, as in Ely Cathedral, the styles of different periods are
blended. There is a noble faith from the first ; but what

shall we say of the savagery ? The enemies of God are to be like wax melting at the fire ; their kings to be driven like snowflakes before the tempest ; God will hunt out His enemies from the depths of the sea, that the feet of His people may be dipped in their blood, and that the tongues of their dogs may be red through the same. That is a primitive style—Norman, with dog-tooth decoration. We are far as yet from the mind of Christ.

But soon there is a change ; the arches begin to soar ; grace and beauty and tenderness appear. God, while losing nothing of His majesty, is seen to be a God of love to His own people. He sets the solitary in families ; He brings the prisoners out of captivity ; He refreshes the weary ; best of all, He Himself daily bears our burden. And now our Lord finds His way into the Psalm. The old triumphant march of Jehovah to the earthly Jerusalem becomes the Lord's Ascension to the heavenly. It is no longer a train of miserable prisoners who are led captive, but captivity itself ; and the Lord, instead of demanding tribute from the conquered, received gifts for men, that the Lord God may dwell among them. The old Norman tower, you see, has fallen ; the great dome has risen to heaven in its place ; and from its summit the Ascended Lord looks down. So the cruel Psalm itself turns missionary. "The Lord gave the word ; great was the company of the preachers"—a glorious mistranslation. The decree for destruction has become the word of the Gospel ; and, instead of savage Hebrew women rejoicing in carnage, we find the Apostles and Evangelists of the Lord.

Thus, from beginning to end, we must now read the Psalm in a new way. The hill of God must mean for us the Catholic Church ; and God's residence there the unfailing presence of the Holy Spirit. The old redemption must yield its place to the new redemption, the old festal worship of Israel to the Church's Eucharistic worship ; and, when the Psalmist speaks of the gracious rain which God sends upon His inheritance, and prays that God will stablish the thing that He has wrought in us, we must think of the great revivals, which the Spirit has granted in the past, not least to the Church of England, and is ready to grant to-day. You see what has taken place. The tide of revelation has come flooding in ; and, though here and there the points of the old cruel rocks are seen above the waters, the "merry and joyful" waves are dancing over them.

II

But it is not chiefly of this that I would speak to you to-day, but of the grand truth which inspired the Psalm as a whole. *"Exurgat Deus"* : our God is a God who can "arise." He is a living, personal, redeeming God ; a God therefore, as the prophet says, who can do for us new things so great and wonderful that the old will not be remembered or come into mind. Most rightly have our Bishops at their Conference called us to a new study of the Christian doctrine of God. We need it, every one of us. Most rightly also do they point out how much there is to help our faith in the modern conception of the universe. But do they not, in dwelling on this, present to us a doctrine of God which is seriously one-sided, and falls short of that of the Bible and the Church ?

The Bible and the Church alike give us two thoughts about God, which we must not separate. On the one hand, God is, as we say, "transcendent" : He is "high and lifted up" above our world of space and time, independent of it, and in no way adequately revealed by it. That is the truth enshrined for us in the noble symbolism of the Apocalypse, to which we listened in the Epistle for to-day. On the other hand, God is, as we say, "immanent" in the world that He has made, the source of its order, its beauty, and its development. Of these two truths it is the first which is the more important, since it is bound up with our belief in redemption, and so with our hope for ourselves and the world.

Now perhaps I do our Bishops an injustice ; but I find

in their words a clearer witness to God's immanence than to His transcendence, to His work in the natural order than to His work in redemption, and so an inadequate grasp of His transforming grace.   May I then try to put the other side before you ?   That revelation of God which made the Psalmists confident even in the darkest days was not given by the order of nature, of which they knew little, or by its progressive development, of which they knew less.   It was a historical revelation, given by God's choice of Israel to be His people, by the mighty Hand which delivered them from slavery, by the great deep of His judgments, and the greater deep of His restoring mercy.   It was, I would suggest, just by the wisdom and power displayed in God's dealings with His people that they learned that Jehovah was no mere tribal god, but the Lord of heaven and earth ; and, when they had learned that, heaven and earth, as well as history, declared His glory.   But the world came second, and not first.   So it should be to-day. Modern science can enrich our thoughts of God, if we keep it in its proper place ; but not if we turn to it first, and seek from it a revelation which it cannot give.

Let me try to make this a little clearer.   We observe first that science can at best speak to us only of God as immanent in the world and the source of its unity and development. It speaks to us of the wisdom, power, and goodness there manifested, but not clearly of any Divine resources beyond. So far as the world can tell us, there are no such resources ; a finite world can only witness to a finite God.   Now this finite God is, in Kipling's phrase, "the God of things as they are."   He cannot break into or transform the existing order, however badly it may need transformation.   No doubt, this order is itself progressive.   The "block universe," the idol of the old Victorian naturalism, is now discredited.   It is widely recognized that much comes into being which is really new, and could not, even with the widest knowledge, have been predicted.   We speak to-day of "creative" or "emergent" evolution ; and that, strictly speaking, is not evolution at all ; the adjective contradicts the noun to which it is attached. In all this there may be a hint of the Divine transcendence, but it does not carry us all the way. The new seems to be strictly conditioned by the old, though not wholly explained by it.

We observe secondly that the world of physical science cannot reveal God's character and purpose, though they are what we need to know. Character can only be fully revealed in dealing with beings who are morally free, and physical science does not tell us how God deals with them. When St. Paul says that the world manifests God's everlasting power and divinity, and should lead us to glorify and to thank Him, his outlook is a wider one than that of Einstein or of Jeans. He is thinking of the world in its relation to man ; of the world in all its beauty and utility, giving us under God "all things richly to enjoy." Einstein and Jeans are concerned with but one aspect of the world, and for their purpose rightly so ; its beauty and utility do not come within their view. What their world reveals of God, as we have been lately told, is that God is a mathematician, and that is not a very thrilling revelation. In a man mathematical proficiency is at least an evidence of industry ; in God it is not even that. Though science tells us of a great universe and of a mysterious universe, neither size nor mystery are certificates of character. A nuisance is not the better for being a great nuisance, nor are we comforted by our inability to understand it.

It is true that the world culminates in man, and that man has spiritual endowments. But what use does he generally make of them ? Man unredeemed does little credit to the God of things as they are. So far from his history being a record of moral and spiritual progress, the latest anthropology seems to show that the most primitive peoples had a far higher idea of God than their more civilized successors. No doubt, when we already know God's character, our thoughts about Him may be enriched by modern science. When we know that He is love, His greatness is a joy to us, and even His mystery a new source of attraction. But we cannot build on science either first or chiefly. Taken by

itself, it is as inadequate to our needs to-day as it has been
in the past.   Indeed, it may even mislead us by suggesting
that God is neither righteousness nor love.

To what then should we turn ?   We should turn where
the Psalmist turned—to the revelation of God in history ;
to those mighty acts of His by which He called the Church
into being and made it the home of His Spirit, and the
witness to His Truth.   We should turn to the Incarnation
and the Cross of Christ ; to the Resurrection and Ascension
and the gift of the Spirit ; to all that God has done for us
in judgment and in mercy all down the Christian ages.
There we shall find, not just the most signal example of
that Divine activity which the world reveals, but the
irruption into the world of a new power from on high, and
that not primarily to carry it forward to a new stage of
development, but to redeem and transform it.   That is
what it needs, as the prophets knew—not evolution, but
revolution.   "Oh ! that Thou wouldest rend the heavens,
that Thou wouldest come down."   And the prophet looks
forward to the fulfilment of his longing.   God "saw that
there was no man, and wondered that there was none to
interpose ; therefore His own arm brought salvation unto
Him ; and His righteousness it upheld Him."

So, too, speaks the New Testament ; it speaks not of
development, but of new birth.   What did St. Paul mean
when he said that the Lord came in the fulness of time ?
Did he mean that the world was now so far advanced that
it was ready for a new step forward ?   A thousand times
no !   He meant that the world was so bankrupt that there
was no hope for it except in the transcendent God ; that
society was so rotten that it was "past feeling" its corrup-
tion ; that the boasted wisdom of the world had brought
no knowledge of God ; that even in Israel the law had
stimulated rebellion rather than got rid of it.   The fullness
of time had come because man's extremity is God's opportunity, and the darkest hour comes just before the dawn.
And what made the Apostolic Church what it was ?   What
explains "the work of faith and labour of love and patience

of hope" that we find there? What made men "merry
and joyful" as they suffered for the Lord's Name? It was
not the sense that a new stage had been reached in human
evolution, but the knowledge that God had arisen; that
the Kingdom had broken through the rent heavens and
the Church was living in a new world. *Exurgat Deus!*
Yes. He has risen indeed, and we with Him. "If God
is for us, who is against us? He that spared not His own
Son, but delivered Him up for us all, how shall He not also
with Him freely give us all things?" Our faith and hope
are now in God, because He has "begotten us again unto a
living hope by the Resurrection of Jesus Christ from the
dead."

III

You see then what I would say to you to-day. Our God
is a transcendent God, sufficient for every need. We
meet again where in past years we have worked and
worshipped together; and some of you perhaps are sadder
men than once you were. You have gone out into the
world; you know better what it is like; and you do not
find things easy. The "enemies" of God are many, and
"they that hate Him" no longer disguise their hate. We
ese the moral standard falling and crime increasing; and
the Church seems weak and drab, a house divided against
itself. Her wings are no silver wings, nor her feathers like
gold. But we are not called to fight and conquer by the
powers we at present possess, but by the powers which our
faith may claim from God, and our faith receive. Lift up
your hearts, not tc the God of things as they are, but to
the God of things as they ought to be, and shall be by His
grace; the God who arises; the God high and lifted up
above the dust and grime of this present world. He is
the "God of whom cometh salvation," the "Lord by whom
we escape death." He sends the gracious rain upon His
inheritance, and refreshes it when it is weary; our forecasts
of the weather are as often mocked as those which we read

in our morning papers. Who in the latter half of the eighteenth century would have foretold an Evangelical revival ? Who in the earlier half of the nineteenth would have foretold a Catholic one ? All the barometers said Very dry,', but the gracious rain came.

So also to-day. If we are faithful, and "faithful" means full of faith, God will not leave us comfortless ; He will come to us. We should "expect great things from God, and attempt great things for God." What we see of Him now is as nothing compared with what we may see ; what He has done for us already, though we rejoice in that, is as nothing compared with what He will do. God, no doubt, is a God of order. We knew that long before science told us of it ; the covenant of the day and the covenant of the night were to Jeremiah the standing witnesses to the reliability of God. But though God is a God of order, He is not a God of routine, set in His ways, and unable to move out of them. If we think that He is that, we shall be men of routine ourselves. We shall be, not round men in square holes ; that is no bad thing to be, since it calls out our powers of self-adaptation. We shall be something worse, "round men in round holes, ever going round and round in them."

What is the revelation which history gives us of the ways of God with men ? It is the revelation of God as the Hound of Heaven, following us down the devious ways that we have chosen, descending low that He may lift us high, adapting Himself to us, since we will not conform ourselves to Him, bringing out of His treasury new stores of power and wisdom and love, making the most, when we will not give Him our best, of the little that we do give Him. And His greatest servants have been like Him. There has been nothing of the doctrinaire about them, nothing of the schoolmaster, nothing of the "take it or leave it" spirit. They have shown something of the adaptability, something of the originality, of the transcendent God. "To the Jews I became as a Jew, that I might gain Jews. To the weak I became weak, that I might gain the weak ;

I am become all things to all men that I may by all means save some."

"*Exurgat Deus !*" May God so arise for you and me, that we may become a little more like Him ! "O God, wonderful art Thou in Thy holy places, even the God of Israel ; He will give strength and power unto His people ; blessed be God."

Trieste

Trieste Publishing has a massive catalogue of classic book titles. Our aim is to provide readers with the highest quality reproductions of fiction and non-fiction literature that has stood the test of time. The many thousands of books in our collection have been sourced from libraries and private collections around the world.

The titles that Trieste Publishing has chosen to be part of the collection have been scanned to simulate the original. Our readers see the books the same way that their first readers did decades or a hundred or more years ago. Books from that period are often spoiled by imperfections that did not exist in the original. Imperfections could be in the form of blurred text, photographs, or missing pages. It is highly unlikely that this would occur with one of our books. Our extensive quality control ensures that the readers of Trieste Publishing's books will be delighted with their purchase. Our staff has thoroughly reviewed every page of all the books in the collection, repairing, or if necessary, rejecting titles that are not of the highest quality. This process ensures that the reader of one of Trieste Publishing's titles receives a volume that faithfully reproduces the original, and to the maximum degree possible, gives them the experience of owning the original work.

We pride ourselves on not only creating a pathway to an extensive reservoir of books of the finest quality, but also providing value to every one of our readers. Generally, Trieste books are purchased singly - on demand, however they may also be purchased in bulk. Readers interested in bulk purchases are invited to contact us directly to enquire about our tailored bulk rates. Email: customerservice@triestepublishing.com

You May Also Like

ISBN: 9780649215652
Paperback: 216 pages
Dimensions: 6.14 x 0.46 x 9.21 inches
Language: eng

The place of women in the church

H. L. Goudge

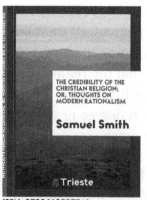

ISBN: 9780649557516
Paperback: 204 pages
Dimensions: 5.83 x 0.43 x 8.27 inches
Language: eng

The Credibility of the Christian Religion; Or, Thoughts on Modern Rationalism

Samuel Smith

www.triestepublishing.com

You May Also Like

ISBN: 9780649690602
Paperback: 114 pages
Dimensions: 6.14 x 0.24 x 9.21 inches
Language: eng

Reports of the Board of Directors and of the Superintendents of the State Hospitals for the Insane at Raleigh, Goldsboro and Morganton, North Carolina

State Hospital of North Carolina

ISBN: 9780649731213
Paperback: 160 pages
Dimensions: 6.14 x 0.34 x 9.21 inches
Language: eng

War Poems, 1898

California Club & Irving M. Scott

You May Also Like

ISBN: 9780649420544
Paperback: 108 pages
Dimensions: 6.14 x 0.22 x 9.21 inches
Language: eng

1807-1907 The One Hundredth Anniversary of the incorporation of the Town of Arlington Massachusetts

Various

ISBN: 9780649194292
Paperback: 44 pages
Dimensions: 6.14 x 0.09 x 9.21 inches
Language: eng

Biennial report of the Board of State Harbor Commissioners, for the two fiscal years commencing July 1, 1890, and ending June 30, 1892

Various

www.triestepublishing.com

You May Also Like

Biennial report of the Board of State Harbor Commissioners for the two fisca years. Commeneing July 1, 1884, and Ending June 30, 1886

Various

ISBN: 9780649199693
Paperback: 48 pages
Dimensions: 6.14 x 0.10 x 9.21 inches
Language: eng

Biennial report of the Board of state commissioners, for the two fiscal years, commencing July 1, 1890, and ending June 30, 1892

Various

ISBN: 9780649196395
Paperback: 44 pages
Dimensions: 6.14 x 0.09 x 9.21 inches
Language: eng

Find more of our titles on our website. We have a selection of thousands of titles that will interest you. Please visit

www.triestepublishing.com